STEVEN RICCHIUTO

UM DISEQUILIBR

{ How America's Great Inflation
Led to the Great Recession }

GREENLEAF
BOOK GROUP PRESS

This publication is designed to provide accurate and authoritative information in regard to the subject matter covered. It is sold with the understanding that the publisher and author are not engaged in rendering professional services. If expert assistance is required, the services of a competent professional should be sought.

Published by Greenleaf Book Group Press
Austin, Texas
www.gbgpress.com

Copyright ©2016 Mizuho Securities USA Inc.

Distributed by Greenleaf Book Group

For ordering information or special discounts for bulk purchases, please contact Greenleaf Book Group at PO Box 91869, Austin, TX 78709, 512.891.6100.

Design and composition by Greenleaf Book Group
Cover design by Greenleaf Book Group

Cataloging-in-Publication data is available.

Print ISBN: 978-1-62634-396-2

eBook ISBN: 978-1-62634-397-9

Part of the Tree Neutral® program, which offsets the number of trees consumed in the production and printing of this book by taking proactive steps, such as planting trees in direct proportion to the number of trees used: www.treeneutral.com

Printed in the United States of America on acid-free paper

16 17 18 19 20 21   10 9 8 7 6 5 4 3 2 1

First Edition

Contents

Preface

The pattern of macroeconomic developments traced out in this book suggests that the world of excess demand that modern macroeconomics is based on no longer exists. Instead, a world of excess supply is the norm, suggesting that many of the macro concepts—like a natural rate of unemployment or an internal speed limit imposed on the domestic economy—are no longer viable. Essentially, this interpretation of the postwar developments suggests that a radical rethink of the levers used by policy makers to influence the economy is already long overdue.

How did we get here? That is the question I kept asking myself as the US economy powered through the long 1991–2001 expansion. Despite a series of exogenous events that were broadly expected to tip the economy into recession, the economy was able to keep pace. In fact, it kept on going—steadily, very much like the Energizer Bunny in the television commercials. The Russian Debacle, the Tequila Crisis, and even the failure of long-term capital management are the key events from this period that were expected to lead to a recession, but they did not. This led me to question why some shocks matter and some do not.

At the time, I was involved with building an investment-grade research department at the securities firm where I was employed. This meant I had to figure out what these credit analysts really did. Back then I tended to be a bit of a quant; I have since realized the limitations of that discipline.

As I learned about credit analysis, however, it became apparent to me that exogenous shocks—like the Russian Debacle—matter only when the flow of liquidity dries up in their wake; and this happens only when balance sheets are stretched. In other words, what looks like a calamitous event becomes calamitous only if businesses or consumers stop spending money—and they don't stop unless their access to funding has been restricted.

This assessment seemed to contradict the general description of how business cycles evolve. The textbook story is that the economy gets overheated, and, as a result, inflation begins to rise. The Fed reacts to the upward pressure on inflation by tightening reserve market conditions—i.e., raising short rates—and the economy slows. A slower economy leads to lower inflation, allowing the Fed to reverse gears, and the whole process starts over again.

The 10-year expansion of the 1990s may have been triggered by the Fed, and yet the recovery that followed was anything but typical. The 2001 recession was the result of a forced corporate-sector balance sheet restructuring. That is when it became apparent that there were two fundamental changes that had coalesced to change the very nature of the business cycle. First, the Reagan supply-side revolution had finally kicked in with the help of Al Gore's Internet; and, as a result, the economy was shifting from being driven by excess demand to excess supply.

The dampening of inflation that followed meant that the business cycle could now last long enough that balance sheets could deteriorate and determine when a recession was possible. In retrospect, this changed dynamic had been evident in the 1991–1993 period as well. But because the credit problems were concentrated in the thrift industry, it had the look and feel of a more traditional cycle—even though it was actually the first of three credit cycles in the postwar period.

The following is not a rigorous economic analysis of the new macro dynamic facing the domestic and global economies. We have not built a model of the economy showing the channels through which the transition to excess supply came about. Rather, it is the observation of someone who has worked in the financial services industry since 1980, and it is presented as a straightforward assessment of the key events that led to the transition from excess demand and inflation cycles to excess supply and credit cycles. Essentially this is the story of the transition from one disequilibrium—excess demand—to another disequilibrium—excess supply.

Along the way, I will also present a simple method for assessing macroeconomic credit quality, along with some suggestions as to how policymakers should alter their behavior in order to better handle new macro dynamics, and what trends to consider to determine whether the economy is beginning to swing back from excess supply. I also make no claim to the originality of anything other than putting the events of the past 30–40 years into perspective; this new assessment is truly my own.

The Financial Crisis of 2007–2009 Reflects a Bigger Fundamental Imbalance

Introduction

Volumes have been written about the financial crisis—the collapse of Lehman Brothers, the government's bailout of AIG and the auto industry, the failure of the Government-Sponsored Enterprises (GSEs), and a number of other domestic financial institutions caught in the grip of a recent economic catharsis. Most of the published analyses tend to deal with either the adverse direct consequences of the crisis or the regulatory failure that allowed the problems to develop in the first place. The social consequences of the crises seem to have received the majority of the media attention. The press focused primarily on the decline in home prices, household wealth, and the resulting rise in structural unemployment in both the construction industry and in the overall economy.

The economic community has also analyzed the social consequences of the crisis, but most studies have tended to look into the effects on bank lending, the linkage between the contraction in credit and the nature of the downturn, and the recovery. Although it is understandable why the analysis of the crisis has gone in this direction, I am afraid people may be missing the forest for the trees. What's lacking—the big-picture "forest," in this case—is the fundamental shift in the economy from excess demand to excess supply and from inflation to credit cycles. Moreover, the perceived regulatory failure that led to the crisis resulted in the Dodd–Frank legislation, which is in the process of fundamentally altering the way banks and the financial services industry will function for years to come. The so-called "Volcker Rule" restrictions on investment banking and the SEC's decision to change the rules governing the net asset value of institutional prime money market mutual funds are additional examples of the regulatory response to the financial crisis, and volumes have been and will continue to be written on these topics.

The growth of household leverage and the lax banking standards that allowed the real estate bubble to inflate have also been studied by academics, policymakers, and the press. This analysis has also been used to support the regulatory reforms that have been advanced. The mismanagement of the auto industry and its financing arms have been well documented by the press; but they've remained largely ignored by economists because the Obama team chose to rescue the industry in light of its vital role in the American economy. The manner in which government policymakers reacted to the crisis is another popular topic with market commentators, economists, and the

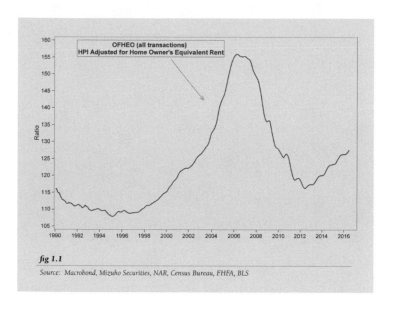

fig 1.1

Source: Macrobond, Mizuho Securities, NAR, Census Bureau, FHFA, BLS

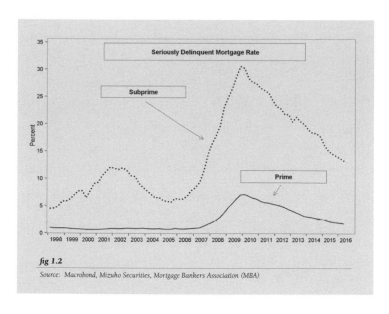

fig 1.2

Source: Macrobond, Mizuho Securities, Mortgage Bankers Association (MBA)

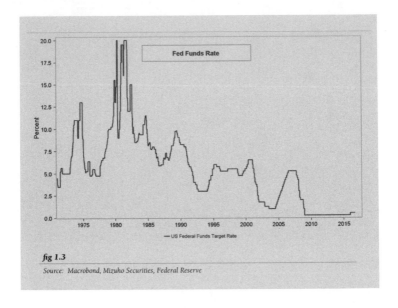

fig 1.3

Source: Macrobond, Mizuho Securities, Federal Reserve

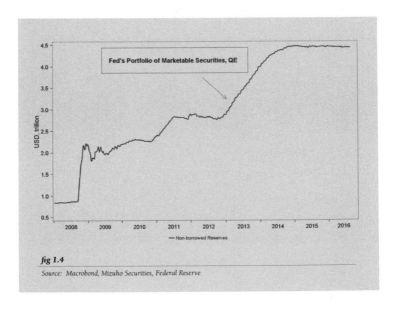

fig 1.4

Source: Macrobond, Mizuho Securities, Federal Reserve

financial press. The Fed's cutting short rates to near zero was followed quickly by targeted liquidity measures; these actions were cobbled together in the midst of the financial crisis to address specific market failures as well as analyses in detail by both the public and private sectors. These programs were eventually replaced by the Fed's large-scale asset purchase program, dubbed "QE," and it's likely the debate over the value of this initiative will rage for years to come.

Almost nothing has been written, however, about *how*, *why*, and *when* the seeds of this crisis were sown. The evolution of the economy, markets, central banking, and government intervention that combined to create the environment in which excess leverage was allowed to be accumulated needs to be assessed to obtain a clear understanding of how the Great Recession and its disappointing recovery came about. It is this excess leverage that eventually crushed the housing, auto, and banking industries. Despite all the new regulations, the economic analyses, financial commentaries, and press coverage of the crisis, unless we understand what precipitated this explosion in leverage and make the appropriate regulatory and policy adjustments, we are likely to repeat the same mistakes again.

To address this deficiency, the analysis in this book will trace the roots of the excess leverage that prompted the financial crisis back to the political and economic climate that emerged immediately after WWII. I will follow these roots through the geopolitical and economic decisions prompted by the Cold War; and I will consider how the weakening of the negotiating power of the unions, the emergence of environmental regulation, and the oil embargoes altered the nature of global competition to the detriment of domestic manufacturers. I will also look at how the Fed's battle against inflation in the 1980s accelerated the major shifts in manufacturing, banking, and financial markets. The surging dollar, the institutionalization of wealth, and the globalization of wealth hastened the growth of the emerging economies. The excessively high short-term interest rates built on the high real rates that followed the war and altered the perceptions of sustainable returns. These developments ultimately shifted the balance between supply and demand in favor of excess supply.

In the early stages of this period, the natural tendency was for excess demand to dominate the business cycle. Since the 1990s, however, the shift to excess supply has tended to dominate. The result has been a dramatic decline in the nominal cost of funding, which, when combined with the blind pursuit of double-digit returns on a three- to six-month basis, has resulted in an economy built on excess leverage and focused on cost cutting and financial engineering to drive earnings. In fact, since the early 1990s there have been only three business cycles, and all have been associated with a run-up in leverage that eventually burst, forcing a deleveraging or, in other words, a credit cycle. Two of these have been consumer and/or housing related, including the latest, which economists call the Great Recession. The credit cycle experienced in 2001 and the dot-com downturn were the result of a forced corporate balance sheet restructuring. If nothing is done to alter domestic competitiveness and to reestablish a better balance between supply and demand by creating good-paying jobs and/or pulling expectations back in line with reality, the next credit cycle could be even deeper than the past three.

Sowing the Seeds of the Imbalance

Demand Pull

The period immediately following WWII was dominated by a confluence of factors, all of which contributed to creating an extended period of excess demand. To avoid the economic and political mistakes made after WWI, the period of repression, which immediately followed the war, eventually morphed into efforts to rebuild Germany and Japan. It became clear after WWII that the way to win peace was through improved quality of life for citizens on both the European and Asian continents and not by extracting never-ending reparations. This drive to reverse the ravages of the war created a surge in demand for everything American and American-made. The fact that our domestic manufacturing and agricultural bases were left not only intact but also greatly expanded, and even more productive, thanks to the war effort, allowed profit-motivated companies to steer the political agenda and seek out beachheads in Europe and Asia as a means of expanding and securing their place as powerful competitors in these regions.

The returning GIs and the programs designed to reintegrate them into society sparked a tremendous surge in demand for consumer products, housing, transportation, and education services. The technological advances pioneered during the war were quickly adapted for peacetime applications, and the explosion in new and existing industries led to a spike in the demand for labor. After an initial period of transition from a wartime to a peacetime economy, real GDP surged and resulted in an explosion in the middle class. High-paying jobs in construction and manufacturing were being created while federal, state, and local governments rushed to build the infrastructure to meet these demands. The rapid expansion of the interstate highway system is an example of this effort to satisfy the demands of a rapidly expanding and more affluent economy. An explosion in household formations and live births also played a big part in shaping the economy in the years following the end of the war. The baby boom, in fact, is one of the most important developments of the postwar period, as it helped set in motion a sustained period of excess demand for goods and services.

Roughly two years after WWII ended, the Cold War began. This set in motion an arms race between the Soviet Union and the West (led by the United States). The industrial policies undertaken in the name of maintaining military preparedness on multiple fronts, as well as permanent military bases in Western Europe and in several countries in Asia, led to rapidly expanding excess demand. President Eisenhower's threat to nationalize the steel industry in the 1950s is an example of how the government and the establishment of a permanent military industrial complex helped to increase aggregate demand and shifted the balance toward a position of excess demand.

Although the Cold War standoff dominated the military focus in Europe, the struggle against Communism expanded into an all-out military conflict on the Korean peninsula and in Southeast Asia, increasing the public sector's demand for both goods and services. At exactly the same time, Lyndon Johnson's "Great Society" experiment and the civil rights movement were increasing the demand for government involvement in expanding social services. This confluence of factors stretched the economy's ability to accommodate this competing demand for a fixed pool of resources.

Strained political relations between Israel and its Arab neighbors boiled over into outright war, and tensions have remained (other than for a short period immediately after the 1978 Carter peace accords were signed between Israel and Egypt). The United States' support for Israel helped to instigate two embargoes by oil-producing Arab nations between 1967 and 1974. These oil-producing nations not only nationalized production facilities that had been built by foreigners on their soil, but they also colluded with other oil-producing nations—OPEC—to fix the price of oil. Crude oil prices, in fact, quadrupled by the end of 1974, rising to over $12 a barrel. The political tensions in the Middle East did not end with the seven-day Yom Kippur War. Instead, the Iranian Revolution and the Iran–Iraq War quickly followed, and crude oil and refined prices moved decidedly higher. Rising crude oil prices quickly rendered a large portion of domestic manufacturing obsolete. This widened the imbalance between demand and supply and put significant upward pressure on prices.

President Kennedy's race to put a man on the moon is another example of how the Cold War influenced the economy of the postwar period. The resulting technological advances sparked innovative new products and new high-wage middle-class jobs, and they helped extend the period of excess demand. Another such example was President Reagan's "Star Wars" missile defense initiative. During the early part of the Cold War, an aggressive push to contain the spread of Communism beyond China led to back-to-back wars in Korea and Vietnam. These long and costly military conflicts, when combined with the rapid expansion of the arms race with the Soviet Union, led to a multiple expansion of the defense industry and the growth of the military industrial complex. The defense industry's demands on domestic manufacturing, natural resources, and skilled labor widened the spread between demand and supply evident in the economy.

Cost Push

The surge in demand for goods and services increased the power of unions as the economic cost of worker unrest increased dramatically and companies embraced collective bargaining as a way to keep factories running. The upward drift in inflation during the first 40 years after the war was amplified in the late 1960s and 1970s by a series of environmental and safety regulations that were imposed on domestic manufacturers. Toxic-waste laws implemented during this period, such as smokestack emissions limits, tailpipe emissions standards, and water pollution laws, added significantly to the cost of doing business; yet they added no benefit to the bottom line. Workplace safety regulations and auto safety laws were also being implemented; these, too, added to the costs of producing goods and services. Health care insurance, Medicare, and Medicaid were all introduced early in the postwar period and then expanded rapidly, resulting in a growing share of the economy dedicated to health services. Adding further to the inflationary pressures were the Cost of Living Adjustment (COLA) clauses built into labor contracts and into Social Security benefits early in the postwar period when the cost of such agreements was perceived to be negligible. Geopolitical developments pushed oil prices even higher to $35 per barrel from essentially $14 per barrel in 1981.

Making matters worse were the industrial policies employed by the US government between 1973 and 1981. Specifically, the oil price controls imposed on domestic oil producers significantly curtailed exploration and production, increasing dependence on higher-cost imported oil. Higher energy costs not only increased the cost of manufacturing, but they also rendered vast amounts of the domestic capital stock obsolete, which in turn contributed to the excess demand situation.

The costs associated with these developments were passed on to the consumer in the form of higher prices, which led to rising wages and the establishment of a wage-price spiral. Rising prices squeezed real household income and the result was increased wage demands by labor unions. The excess demand environment weakened management's ability to resist, and cost-push inflation compounded the problem generated by demand-pull inflation pressures. Inflation ratcheted upward of 14% in the late 1980s from just 1.5% in the 1950s.

Shifting Dynamics of Supply and Demand

The great inflation period of the late 1970s and the Reagan supply-side revolution played key roles in moving the economy from excess demand to excess supply. The Reagan tax cut was justified under the theory that lower tax rates boosted investment and created noninflationary growth. We can argue all day about the empirical support for the Laffer curve; however, the resulting increase in government bonds that was associated with the reduction in marginal tax rates led to a sharp rise in real interest rates. A higher real rate and a double-digit inflation premium resulted in not only long-term government bond rates above 14%, but also the Fed's shift in monetary policy from interest rates to non-borrowed reserves targeting.

Targeting the money supply resulted in a dramatic increase in short-term rates. In fact, the federal funds rate actually traded up to 26% one night. The Volcker tightening inverted the yield curve as short rates rose to a high of 20% in March 1980. This dynamic accelerated the institutionalization of wealth as investors pulled money out of passbook savings accounts and bank CDs and funneled these proceeds into money market mutual funds. These relatively new investment products promised both high returns and liquidity, leading to a multiple expansion in the mutual fund industry. As the economy slumped into the 1981–1982 recession and inflation began to slow, the Fed began to cut rates and the financial services industry shifted gears to take advantage of new opportunities created by the institutionalization of wealth.

Mutual fund managers reacted quickly to the declining rate environment by talking up the benefits of their equity and bond mutual funds. The logic was simple and straight-forward. Mutual fund managers could search out companies that had bloated management, excess staff, and inefficient collections of business and use shareholder activism to increase the return to investors in their funds. The game plan was to reward companies whose management focused on achieving strong quarterly earnings targets through cost cutting, strategic M&A, jettisoning underperforming product lines and businesses, and, when necessary, using financial engineering to boost earnings per share.

As money managers ran out of easy domestic companies to restructure, the focus began to shift in the 1980s to overseas companies, and the globalization of the financial market kicked into high gear. Companies and CEOs were rewarded for shifting production overseas or creating strategic alliances that could help provide product to domestic consumers at a lower cost. The export-to-growth model was exported to Latin America, Southeast Asia, Eastern Europe (following the collapse of the Berlin Wall), and eventually to China as well as the African continent. The cumulative result of this global push to industrialize was a shift in the balance between supply and demand.

This shift was further exaggerated by the demographics of an aging population and a slowing in population growth in developed countries. The institutionalization and the globalization of wealth created a world of excess supply of tradable goods, and, in the process, turned the tide on inflation.

Economists tend to credit the disinflation that followed in the wake of the 1981–1982 recession as being a result of increased central bank credibility in fighting inflation.

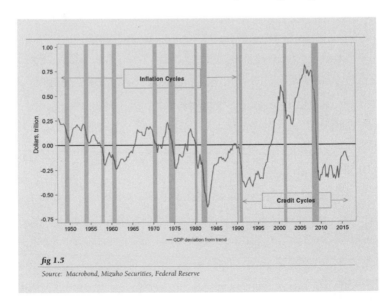

fig 1.5

Source: Macrobond, Mizuho Securities, Federal Reserve

Although it would be nice to assume that inflation expectations could be influenced that easily, the macroeconomic and financial market dynamics of the period combined with the investment community's adaptive expectations are more likely to have caused the reduction in inflation and gradual decline in inflation expectations that resulted. In essence, a fundamental shift from excess demand to excess supply of tradable goods exerted downward pressure on inflation, which was reinforced by the search for double-digit quarterly returns.

Excess Demand and Inflation Cycles

In an economy skewed toward excess demand, inflation tends to dominate the business cycle. Specifically, as the economy heats up, demand is pulled up relative to the available supply of goods and services, and prices begin to rise. Initially, rising prices increase corporate profitability as nominal wages lag, resulting in a decline in real wages. This development causes companies to increase hiring, which further widens the excess demand situation. To retain and attract qualified workers in a tightening labor market, companies eventually bid up nominal wages. Rising nominal wages then return real wages to their original position and labor demand contracts, but the excess demand situation remains. At this point, the general level of prices is higher, as is the nominal wage rate.

If policymakers attempt to maintain the increase in output and the decline in the jobless rate by applying either fiscal or monetary stimulus, a wage-price spiral is established. The Nixon wage and price controls were sparked by this adverse series of developments, and despite the intellectual appeal of the program, it only exacerbated the wage-price spiral as a result of its poor execution.

Even without a wage-price spiral, rising prices eventually become a problem for the economy, as inflation tends to rise more quickly than wages. As the pressure to slow inflation increases, policymakers are forced to tighten monetary conditions in order to slow the economy. Higher short rates cause banks to pull back on lending, and the increased cost of short-term funding reduces aggregate demand. This process pulls demand back toward supply, and inflation cools.

The key thing to recognize about an inflation cycle is that there is nothing fundamentally wrong in the economy. The problem is that the economy has been running above its internal speed limit, and this imbalance caused inflation to accelerate. As such, the contraction in credit orchestrated by the Fed is artificially induced and can be quickly reversed once the inflation cycle is broken. These are the V-shaped business cycles of the postwar period. Inflation cycles by their nature tended to be short in duration. The average cycle upturn lasted between 3 and 4 years, while the downturns were only 11 months on average.

Excess Supply and Credit Cycles

In an economy skewed toward excess supply, inflation no longer determines the business cycle. Instead, it is the expansion and contraction of credit within the economy that determine the ebbs and flows. As a result, balance sheets determine relative performance as well as the overall health of the economy. When balance sheets are generally strong and liquidity is flowing, the economy tends to grow and can deal with external shocks to the system without skipping a beat. When balance sheets are weak, any shock to the system, either domestic or international, will cause liquidity to dry up and the economy to slip into a recession.

Credit recessions are very different from inflation cycle recessions. In an inflation cycle, nothing is inherently wrong in the economy. The economy just overheats; and once the Fed tightens credit, the economy slows and inflation cools. The economy is then ready to resume its upward trajectory as soon as monetary policy becomes more accommodative. In a credit cycle, one or more sector balance sheets have been compromised; and, as a result, the smooth flow of liquidity in the economy breaks down. As liquidity contracts, the economy slides into a recession; and not until balance sheets are restructured can the economy begin to recover. Because balance sheets take time to restructure, the recovery process can be rather lengthy. The process of deteriorating and then repairing balance sheets takes time, resulting in a lengthy expansion and a protracted recovery phase. The three credit-induced business cycles of the postwar period have lasted almost 8 years on average, with the longest recovery/expansion phase lasting 10 years.

The economy can generally be broken down into four major balance sheets: public sector, household sector, nonfinancial corporate sector, and banking. The public sector comprises federal, state, and local entities. Although there are clear blemishes on the government sector's balance sheets, we are basically looking at an investment-grade sector. The power to tax individuals, households, and corporations is enormously valuable from the perspective of a rating agency looking at credit quality. The market tends to agree with this interpretation, as reflected in the limited interest-rate premium imposed on government borrowers. The liquidity provided to not-so-healthy public entities shows that the power to tax is a valuable asset.

On the other hand, household balance sheets and nonfinancial corporate balance sheets are both evaluated the same way. There are three fatal sins of leverage. There is excess leverage, duration structure, and a debt burden. The more leveraged households or companies are, the shorter the duration of their liabilities are, or the higher their debt burden is (i.e., their cost of interest), the more likely creditors are to withhold funding, triggering a credit event. The banking industry's balance sheet can be summarized in just two key indicators of financial health: nonperforming loan balances (or those deficient 30 days or more) and the coverage ratio. The higher the nonperforming loan rate, the less willing banks are to lend and vice versa. The coverage ratio is the relative position of loan loss reserves held by banks to their level of nonperforming loans. Banks look at the coverage ratio both directionally and in an absolute sense. A rising ratio is preferred to a declining one. The higher the coverage ratio, the more willing banks are to extend liquidity to the economy.

The First Three Postwar Credit Cycles

The 1990–1991 contraction was the first credit cycle of the postwar period that was a banking-related downturn. The collapse of the thrift industry in the late 1980s and its adverse effects on the housing industry, and on bank lending in general, caused a deep and prolonged downturn in the economy. Bank nonperforming loan balances shot up as a result, and the government was forced to create the Resolution Trust Corporation (RTC) to warehouse the loans of failed home lenders. The government's direct involvement in restructuring loans and unloading foreclosed assets took several years, and the recovery was characterized as a jobless recovery until 1993. Another unique aspect of the contraction and the early phase of the recovery was the high level of real long-term rates. This was a legacy of the Reagan–Bush era of large and rising budget deficits. The tax hike initiative and health care debate launched by the Clinton administration in its first 100 days resulted in a dramatic decline in long-term rates. Declining long-term rates accelerated the government's efforts to restructure the housing market, which included a more active role for the federal agencies in providing liquidity to the housing market. The result was an economy that gained traction in 1994 and expanded through the rest of the decade, principally as a result of government intervention in the housing markets. The monetary policy stimulus provided by the Federal Open Market Committee (FOMC) may have been responsible for the economy finding a bottom in early 1991, but the Fed's interest rate policy was not well equipped to deal with a market failure.

The 2001 recession was short and shallow. The cause behind this credit cycle was the collapse of the commercial paper market on the back of several high-profile corporate bankruptcies. In the run-up to Y2K and the rapid expansion of the technology industry and the dot-com bubble, companies were being rewarded for growth, not for good financial practices. The result was an inappropriate reliance on short-term funding. The corporate sector in general became reliant on short-term funding, even for long-term development programs. When these highly levered companies ran into funding difficulties in the commercial paper market, investors suddenly realized that this reliance on short-term debt was broad based, and the result was a credit squeeze. As companies rushed to extend the duration of their liabilities, earnings expectations collapsed, and the dot-com bubble burst. The 9/11 terrorist attacks prompted an aggressive easing by the Fed and the large marginal tax cut by the George W. Bush administration. These developments jump-started the corporate restructuring into long-term term liabilities, and investors lined up to buy this new supply; because other than a duration problem, the nonfinancial corporate balance sheet was largely healthy. As a result, the downturn was only nine months long—and yet the recovery was still drawn out, because even the highly liquid domestic corporate bond market still had internal rigidities, as well as underwriting and capacity constraints.

The 2007–2009 credit cycle is the most recent credit-induced decline in the economy. This downturn was deep in terms of lost output and long in duration. The recovery was also drawn out because more than one balance sheet was involved, as well as more than one key industry. The collapse in the housing market triggered a significant deterioration in the household balance sheet, which was subsequently amplified by the failure of two of the Big Three domestic auto manufacturers. As households ran into financial difficulty, they began to default on their mortgage obligations, and homes depreciated in value. The result was a collapse in banking activity, the failure of a major domestic insurance company, and two large financial services companies. In retrospect, it is clear that bank underwriting standards had been lowered too much under the Clinton administration's rush to boost home ownership. The result was that households bought "more home" than they could afford under the premise that prices only went up.

The tight links between problems in household balance sheets and the problems in the banking, insurance, and financial services industries deepened the downturn in the overall economy through a negative feedback loop. As banks rushed to cut back on lending and seized defaulted properties, home prices declined further and foreclosures increased. This then resulted in more homeowners being upside down in their mortgages—owing more than their homes were worth—thus extending the negative feedback loop. The collapse in the housing market spilled over into other markets and into the overseas banking industry as well. Foreign banks participated in the US housing boom directly through mortgages they originated, the asset-backed securities they bought, and/or their ownership of Federal agency debt (Fannie Mae, Freddie Mac, FHA), all of which plummeted in value as the primary and secondary markets dried up.

The collapse in the demand for credit outpaced the decline in official short rates, and as rates approached the zero lower bound, the FOMC was forced to execute nontraditional, quantitative easing (QE) in the hopes of stabilizing asset prices. The Fed kicked off QE by buying mortgages and agency securities and eventually broadened the program to include government bonds. The result was a multiple expansion of the Fed's balance sheet to $4.5 trillion. As the Fed's portfolio expanded, long-term rates declined and yield-hungry investors shifted out the credit curve into investment-form high-grade corporate bonds to high-yield bonds and domestic equities. The increase in liquidity in the financial markets spilled into the housing market as REITs rushed into the real estate own-to-rent business. These nontraditional participants in the single-family market reversed the direction of home prices and set the stage for banks to begin the long process of quantifying the problem and starting to restructure and write down the bad debt.

The foreclosure process exposed poor bank underwriting practices and documentation procedures. The result was a political backlash against banks and the passage of the now infamous Dodd–Frank legislation. The imposition of new capital requirements, additional accounting standards, and more complicated compliance regulations increased the stress on banks struggling to restructure while paying huge fines to the federal government. This confluence of factors slowed the process of balance sheet restructuring. Passage of the Obama tax hike in the middle of the recovery further hindered the recovery and helped establish a shallow growth trajectory that lasted several years into the upturn in the cycle.

Managing for Earnings

The institutionalization and globalization of wealth set the stage for a fundamental shift in the economy that is very evident today: the shift from a world of excess demand to a world of excess supply. With this shift came the transition from inflation determining the business cycle to credit quality determining the business cycle, i.e., the timing of recessions and recoveries. Another important development that aided this transition in business cycle dynamics was a philosophical change in corporate boardrooms to a culture of managing for quarterly earnings instead of for long-term growth. This was a major shift, as in the years immediately following WWII, companies were focused on long-term growth. America's dominance in technology, mass production, and quality allowed companies to generate almost monopolistic profits and build large, complex, horizontally and vertically integrated companies. As overseas competition increased, the regulatory environment tightened, raw material prices rose, interest rates rose, and the dollar depreciated. This long-term growth strategy led to companies that were bloated and ineffective. As a result, smart CEOs quickly learned that the equity market would reward management that focused on shareholder value. This led to the evolution from a long-term management style to one that focused on a three-month earnings target.

By the 1970s, companies tended to have several layers of management that could be trimmed, assembly lines and distribution channels that could be streamlined and/or automated, and product lines that could be repositioned, refocused, or rebranded to boost earnings. The Reagan-era push to deregulate the airline and the telecommunication industries as well as to scale back the power of big unions helped increase the flexibility of the labor markets. His firing of the air traffic controllers was a high-profile attack on union power that set the stage for companies to find ways to cut labor costs in an effort to increase market share and boost earnings. Eventually

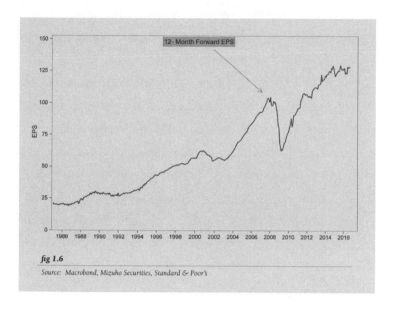

fig 1.6

Source: *Macrobond, Mizuho Securities, Standard & Poor's*

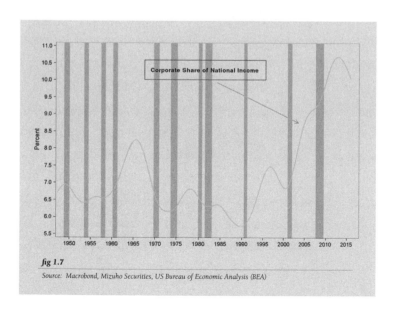

fig 1.7

Source: *Macrobond, Mizuho Securities, US Bureau of Economic Analysis (BEA)*

companies had to seek overseas sources for raw materials and finished products to keep lowering their costs in order to achieve aggressive earning targets.

As more and more companies shifted to this operating strategy, the ability to differentiate on anything other than price diminished. These developments helped bring about the export-to-growth model for the developing world, which subsequently resulted in a world of excess supply. Excess supply limits corporate pricing power. Today's combination of financial engineering and the focus on cost cutting is a direct result of companies that are being managed to maximize shareholder value by targeting double-digit earnings in what is now a low-single-digit world.

The difficulty in accomplishing the goal of double-digit earnings growth in today's domestic and global economic environments has also led to the extensive use of financial engineering to boost earnings. Typically, financial engineering is thought of as share buybacks and dividend increases. Share buybacks are designed to increase earnings per share by reducing the supply of shares outstanding. A dividend increase is another way in which to return money to shareholders to drive up the share price. Leveraged M&A is also used to unlock shareholder value as companies are either split into component parts to boost returns or combined in order to generate synergies. Unfortunately, when all companies employ the same strategies, it is harder for any one company to stand out. Additionally, the constraint on wages imposed by this corporate model also works to limit aggregate demand, which causes additional downward pressure on prices and limits top-line revenue, thus creating a negative feedback loop.

Conclusions

The world of excess supply has been building for more than 25 years and is now eerily similar to that which existed between the Great Depression and WWII. The Great Recession of 2007–2009 was followed by an unprecedented decline in the labor force participation rate as discouraged workers exited the labor force. The economy has had difficulty gaining sustainable momentum as the banking industry and the household sector have been linked together in a forced balance sheet restructuring. Disinflationary forces have also surfaced, not only in the market for tradable goods, but also in the commodity markets. These factors are fully consistent with an economy that is confronting an excess supply imbalance and policymakers who are relying on monetary policy to correct a situation that it is ill equipped to counter. The relative ineffectiveness of monetary policy is evident in the fact that the FOMC has been forced to execute nontraditional policy by expanding its balance sheet. This foray into fiscal policy by the Fed is less effective than more traditional fiscal policy tools, because it works indirectly through a banking industry that is besieged by new regulatory and capital requirements.

The banking industry has also been preoccupied with restructuring nonperforming loans. Supply imbalances in the developed world are another indicator that this time, something is different. Japan has been struggling to exit deflation for years, and the jury is still out on "Abenomics." The government debt crisis in Europe exacerbated the financial problem confronting the southern members of the European Union. The result has been the accumulation of deflationary forces in most EU countries. Even China is facing a rate of wholesale price decline exceeding that of Japan.

Despite the fundamental imbalance in supply both domestically and overseas, economists and policymakers still appear to be viewing the economy from an excess demand perspective. This reveals a lack of understanding of the fundamental change in the economy over the postwar period, which is evident in the fact that the last three business cycles have been credit-motivated, not inflation-motivated.

Demand-Pull Inflation and the Devastating Effect of Modern Warfare

The world of excess demand that followed in the wake of WWII triggered a series of policy changes that would eventually transit the economy into today's excess supply position. However, it is important to understand how the war reshaped the economy and set the stage for the acceleration in inflation that would prove to be the catalyst for an expansion in the supply side of the economy. The economy would experience a combination of demand-pull and cost-push inflation during the 35–40 years that immediately followed the war; to counter these forces, policymakers would have to rethink their views on both monetary and fiscal policy.

To understand how WWII contributed to a world of excess

demand for 35 to 40 years after the hostilities, it is necessary to recognize not only the radical nature of the military campaigns waged, but also the scope of the destruction caused by the conflict. Prior to WWII, battles were typically fought on open fields or on the open water. Civilian populations and basic infrastructure tended to be spared the immediate consequences of the battle, although crimes against humanity and pillaging were always a part of war. WWII, by contrast, was fought on land, sea, and air. This new dimension allowed the combatants to target not only their opponent's army and navy but also their enemy's manufacturing, transportation, and population centers. The destructive power of a mechanized war started to surface at the end of WWI, and during the 21 years between WWI and WWII, the ability to destroy was raised from an art to a science. In addition to large pitched land and naval battles, WWII was fought house to house in every village, town, and city, leaving nothing but total devastation in its wake.

The nature of warfare also evolved dramatically during WWII with the introduction of more advanced tanks, planes, ships, submarines, rockets, and finally the nuclear bomb. The technology of war tended to be fairly static in prior wars. To win a mechanized war, however, combatants have to destroy their enemy's military capabilities, their ability to rearm, and the will to fight. The addition of airplanes and missiles allowed military force to be projected far from the battlefield, essentially right into the enemy's backyard. As a result, the destructive nature of the war was felt across three continents.

Mechanized Destruction and Postwar Repression

To illustrate how much more destruction was unleashed during WWII, estimates place casualties from WWI at 10 million dead, of which 7 million were civilian. Approximately 21 million people were wounded, with 7.7 million either missing or imprisoned.

By contrast, over 60 million people died in WWII. Estimates of total deaths attributed to the Second World War range from 50 million to 80 million, of which 38 million to 55 million are assumed to be civilian. Some 13 million to 20 million of these civilian deaths appear to have been from war-related diseases or famine. Looked at from a different perspective, nearly one in ten Germans died during the war, and about 30% of their army was killed. Additionally, some 27 million Russians were killed during the course of WWII. Between 10 million and 20 million Chinese perished, more than 70% civilian. The Japanese lost about 2 million soldiers and upwards of 1 million civilians, or 4% of its population. Even the UK is estimated to have lost 15% of its population as a result of the war. On average, some 30,000 people were killed each day during the six years of the conflict. Despite the magnitude of the statistics, the true devastation of WWII is best expressed by the newsreel footage of Dresden, Berlin, and the destruction produced by the two nuclear bombs dropped on Japan that brought the Pacific War to its end.

The destructive nature of the war was amplified in the initial phase of the postwar period, not just by the division of Europe into two separate blocs but also by the reparations imposed. Germany was forced to pay reparations to the United Kingdom, France, and the Soviet Union. These reparations were in the form of dismantled factories, forced labor, and coal. The US and Britain also pursued a program of "intellectual reparations" designed to extract all of the technology, scientific know-how, and patents they could from Germany. Financial reparations were also extracted from Italy, Romania, Hungary, Bulgaria, and Finland in accordance with the Treaty of Paris.

Between April 1945 and July 1947, the official US policy toward Germany was to provide no assistance other than to keep the German people from starvation. The initial industrial plan for Germany signed in 1946 called for a 50% reduction in its heavy industry, or the destruction of 1,500 manufacturing plants. The goal was to destroy Germany's ability to wage war again. By 1950, it is estimated that equipment was removed from over 700 factories, and steel production was cut by 6.7 million tons. By 1951, the dismantling of German industry ended as it became clear that a sustainable recovery in Europe could not take hold without the reconstruction of the West German manufacturing base. The Cold War amplified the need for a propitious Western Europe, as the focus of the US military had shifted from an army of occupation to a front-line defensive force against the growing conventional and nuclear military capabilities of the USSR, and the emergence of Communist China as a major power in Asia.

A comparable policy of deindustrializing Japan was implemented immediately after the war with the stated goal of reducing the Japanese standard of living to that which prevailed from 1930–1934. However, the costs of providing emergency aid to Japan to avoid starvation led to a 1948 decision to begin the reconstruction of the Japanese economy. The combination of war-related destruction and postwar reparations dramatically reduced the ability of the global economy to produce manufactured goods and capital equipment. The establishment of the Cold War arms race simply exaggerated this imbalance, as did the military operations required to support the wars on the Korean peninsula as well as in Vietnam. The need to defend against the growing threat of Communism required the full focus of the military, making political stability and economic growth in Japan a domestic security issue.

War	Deaths	Date	Location
World War II	40–60M	1939–1945	Worldwide
World War I/Great War	20M	1914–1918	Worldwide
Korean War	1.2M	1950–1953	Korea

fig 2.1

Source: Congressional Research Service

Birth of the Military Industrial Complex

The counterbalancing factors at work, at least through the 1945–1965 period, were the reorganization and expansion of the US economy after the war and the speed at which domestic manufacturers shifted back to peacetime production. Although many people thought the US would inevitably be brought into the war as the conflict spread through Europe between 1939 and 1941, the federal government's leadership in the area of preparedness prior to Pearl Harbor altered the economy in profound ways. Although the automobile industry resisted transitioning to aircraft production and development prior to Pearl Harbor, the conversion was completed in 1942, and by the next year, the production of aircrafts increased dramatically. Merchant shipbuilding transitioned very early on under the direction of the US Maritime Commission, a New Deal agency designed to revive shipbuilding during the Depression. Between 1930 and 1936, only 71 ships were produced domestically. Between 1938 and 1940, the Commission-sponsored shipyards built 106 ships, and almost the same number in 1941 alone. Ships were needed to ferry goods to Great Britain, France, and other allies in Europe under the "Lend-Lease" program.

The federal government's involvement in the business of the private sector was greatly expanded by the mobilization for WWI, and then expanded during the New Deal period following the start of the Great Depression. However, it reached new heights during WWII and never fully returned to prior

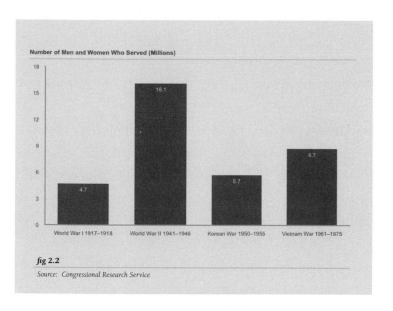

fig 2.2

Source: Congressional Research Service

	Years of War Spending		Peak Year of War Spending	
	Total Military Cost of War in Millions/Billions of Dollars	War Cost % GDP in Peak Year of War		Total Defense % GDP in Peak Year of War
World War I	**1917–1921**		**1919**	
Current Year $	20 billion	13.6%		14.1%
Constant FY2011$	334 billion			
World War II	**1941–1945**		**1945**	
Current Year $	296 billion	35.8%		37.5%
Constant FY2011$	4,104 billion			
Korea	**1950–1953**		**1952**	
Current Year $	30 billion	4.2%		13.2%
Constant FY2011$	341 billion			
Vietnam	**1965–1975**		**1968**	
Current Year $	111 billion	2.3%		9.5%
Constant FY2011$	738 billion			
Persian Gulf War	**1990–1991**		**1991**	

fig 2.3

Source: Congressional Research Service

levels after the war. Although the US did not follow the central planned efforts that dominated in Europe, the military services did have the ability to limit the production of consumer-related products and directed production through their procurement processes.

One way of assessing the effect of the war on the economy is to compare the growth in the economy to that of defense spending. Between 1940 and 1945, the US economy expanded by 71.1%, while defense spending, as a percent of the overall economy, grew from just 1.6% to over 37%. It has been estimated that federal defense spending increased to over $64.5 billion in just five years from $1.7 billion in 1940, after adjusting for inflation. A more detailed cost estimate compiled by the Congressional Research Service suggests the cost of WWII was $296 billion from 1941–1945, or $4.1 trillion in 2008 dollars. This represented 37.5% of GDP during the peak year of the war. Although there was a peace dividend immediately following the war, the advent of the Cold War–inspired arms race and the permanent military presence in both Western Europe and in Asia led to a permanent military industrial complex.

Cold War Turns Hot

The Korean conflict, often referred to as the Forgotten War, was the first time East and West faced off during the postwar period in a military conflict to expand or defend their sphere of influence. The Korean peninsula had been ruled by Japan since 1910, but after the war, the country was split at the 38th parallel by Truman and Stalin, and two separate governments were installed. Korea, unlike the other countries occupied by Japan prior to or during the war, had no government waiting in exile to return to power once the fighting stopped. The Stalin-backed Kim Il-sung regime and the US-backed presidency of Syngman Rhee did not recognize the other as the legitimate government of the peninsula.

Neither superpower had intended the division of the peninsula to be permanent at the outset. The government in the North, however, began an intensive military buildup, supported by the USSR, immediately after the UN created an independent South Korea in early 1948, when it became clear that a formula for a unified Korea could not be found. By mid-1950, Kim Il-sung convinced Stalin that it was time for a military solution to be imposed, and on June 25, 1950, North Korea launched its offensive across the 38th parallel. The initial success of the North Korean army forced direct US military intervention. Active involvement in the war, first by Russian pilots flying support operations for the North Korean army and eventually by Chinese troops, led to an eventual expansion of US ground troops to more than 256,000 by May 1951 and the commitment of some 1,400 aircraft and significant artillery and logistic support from the US Navy.

UN involvement in the conflict also meant additional military support from the UK and Canada. With the realization in 1951 that neither side was going to win militarily, a Demilitarized Zone was established, and in July 1953 a UN commission was set up to supervise the armistice. It is estimated that about 2.5 million people lost their lives due to the conflict. The additional demands on the US military led to a further expansion of the US military industrial complex as a substantial military presence was to be maintained to police the peace. Although the cost of the Korean War pales in comparison to that of WWII, the Congressional Research Service estimates the conflict cost $30 billion between 1950 and 1953, or $320 billion in 2008 dollars. This amounted to 13.2% of GDP in 1952.

A second proxy war began to heat up shortly after hostilities in Korea ended in a stalemate. Following the 1954 collapse of the French colonial administration in Vietnam, the communist government in the North sought to unify the country. The South was closely aligned with the US and Western Europe, while the North was ideologically aligned with China and the USSR. The French occupation had been heavily supported by the US government, and the civil war was seen as an ideological struggle against the spread of Communism. As a result, US military advisors had been present in the South through the 1950s, but by 1965, active combat units had been deployed. In just four years, more than 500,000 military units were stationed in South Vietnam as the war spread to both Laos and Cambodia in the early 1970s. The Chinese and Soviet support for the North escalated the human and Defense Department costs of the war, and support began to decline among the voting public. By 1973, US combat troops were withdrawn, and the government in the South fell just two years later in 1975.

The US military has identified more than 58,000 soldiers who lost their lives during the war, while the Vietnamese estimated that civilian and military casualties on both sides of the civil war totaled more than 3 million. The cumulative cost of the war for the US government has been estimated at $111 billion over the ten years of the war, or 9.5% of 1968 GDP. This would amount to more than half a trillion in 2008 dollars.

The Berlin Wall and the Cuban Missile Crisis

Two other important milestones of the Cold War period that further increased aggregate demand, and positioned the government in direct competition with the private sector for the use of limited resources, were the building of the Berlin Wall in August 1961 and the Cuban Missile Crisis in the fall of 1962. To stem the mass emigration of young, trained professionals out of East Germany, the Soviet-backed government of East Germany erected a wall around West Berlin, cutting it off completely from the rest of East Germany. It has been estimated that by the time the wall was built, upwards of 2.5 million people had fled to the West for a better life. The Soviet Union saw East Germany as simply the spoils of war and repatriated most of its assets back to Russia after the war. The sharp divergence between the economic growth in the West and the deteriorating relative living conditions in the East were the cause of the emigration. Before the Wall was built, the East German government had repeatedly attempted to seize control of the western half of the city, and Khrushchev even threatened the use of nuclear weapons over the issue. This heightened tensions substantially during the Cold War period.

These tensions almost boiled over into an all-out potential nuclear war in the summer of 1962. After the failed Bay of Pigs invasion by US-backed Cuban refugees, Fidel Castro and Nikita Khrushchev reached a secret agreement to deploy Soviet nuclear missiles on the island to deter any further attempts to overthrow the communist regime. The Soviets were also unhappy with the recent deployment of US Jupiter missiles in Turkey, a NATO ally. The crisis escalated quickly, and at one point, the Joint Chiefs of Staff raised the level of military readiness to DEFCON-3 as the navy began accelerated plans for an attack on Cuba. The Soviets responded with a statement that the planned US blockade of the island would be seen as an "act of aggression." Although nuclear war was averted by a last-minute diplomatic solution in which the Russian missiles were removed in exchange for promises that the US would not attack Cuba, the postwar arms race accelerated in its wake.

Although neither of these incidents led to a significant increase in manpower deployed overseas, they did lead to increased international tensions, demands for more effective military capabilities, and increased spending on deterrent weapons systems. The arms race that followed eventually bankrupted the USSR and resulted in an explosive increase in the US budget deficit under President Reagan.

However, the expanded US military involvement in the purchase of weapons and the research and development of entirely new weapons systems added significantly to the government's demands on the economy as far back as 1957. It became clear that the Cold War competition between the US and the USSR would take place not only on Earth, but also in outer space. This added an entirely new dimension to the government's demands on raw materials, manufacturing capacity, and intellectual talent. The arms race led to a push for newer and faster ways of projecting force into potential combat areas, the development of the Intercontinental Ballistic Missile System (ICBMS), the development of newer and faster spy planes (SR-71 Blackbird to replace the U2), and the development and deployment of satellites to monitor troop and equipment movements around the world—24 hours a day.

Space Race

Perhaps the most notable of these pushes into new technology was the race to put a man on the moon. Following the historic Soviet Union launch of *Sputnik* 1 in October 1957, Congress passed a series of massive federal aid-to-education measures. Science became a priority in schools and universities. The Soviets also put the first man in space in 1961, which prompted President Kennedy to tell a joint session of Congress in May 1961 that the US would land a man on the moon and bring him home before the end of the decade. Eight years later there were six single-man Mercury launches; a two-man Gemini program that included the first spacewalk and the first docking of two spacecraft; and a three-man Apollo 11 program that landed two men on the moon. A total of 400,000 employees working for 20,000 companies contributed to the Apollo program.

Many of today's technological advances can trace their origins back to the space program. In fact, technology developed by NASA filtered down into the rest of the economy through commercial application in robotics, computer hardware, computer software, nanotechnology, aeronautics, transportation, and health care. Companies like Intel may never have existed if not for the space program, which extended well beyond the Apollo program into the Shuttle program and the International Space Station. During the 30 years of the Shuttle program the government spent nearly $200 billion on 131 launches. It is estimated that as much as seven or eight dollars in goods and services is still produced for every dollar invested in NASA. The result was a significant increase in demand for goods, services, and labor, helping to extend the world of excess demand.

Baby Boom

Increased employment initiated by the war effort continued well into the postwar period as the Cold War and the arms race between the East and the West continued right through the fall of the Berlin Wall in November 1989. Increased mobility, higher household income, and the explosion in the number of middle-class households were the key developments of a world where excess demand dominated the economic landscape. The associated demand for housing, household appliances, autos, and leisure-related spending expanded the level of demand worldwide, while Europe and Asia rebuilt their infrastructures and manufacturing capabilities under the relative peace that the Cold War standoff established. The result was the Golden Age of the US and Western economies that dominated the 1950s and 1960s. The postwar prosperity produced an important demographic shift that is still reverberating through the domestic and global economies—the postwar baby boom. Following the end of the war, the birthrate spiked in almost every major economy as the rebuilding effort led to increased prosperity, especially in the West.

When the war ended in 1945, returning US veterans had a lot of catching up to do as they reintegrated into society and the economy. To help, Congress passed the GI Bill of Rights. This legislation encouraged investment in education and home ownership by providing low-interest loans to veterans so they could grab their piece of the American dream. These twenty-something veterans married, started families, went to college, and moved to planned communities on the outskirts of big cities. This led to the development of the suburbs which, in turn, required increased infrastructure spending on roads, mass transit, schools, hospitals, power generation, and water and sewer systems—all of which supported increased employment, especially in white-collar jobs that exacerbated the excess demand situation.

The baby boom numbers are staggering. In the US, more babies were born in the 7 years after 1948 than in the previous 30 years. In 1946, live births in the US surged from 222,721 in January to 339,499 in just 9 months. It is estimated that by the end of the 1940s some 32 million babies were born. By contrast, just 24 million had been born in the prior decade. In 1954, annual births broke the 4 million barrier and did not fall below that level until 1965. The surge in births that followed the war was the direct result of a sharp rise in the marriage rate, a decline in the age people got married, and an increase in family size. According to demographers, the average woman bore 3.09 babies in 1950; but this increased to a peak of 3.77

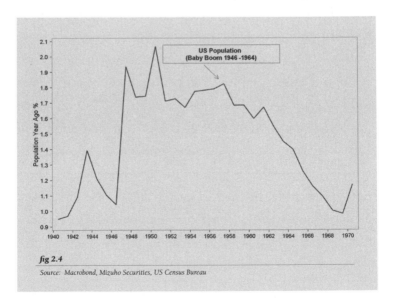

fig 2.4

Source: Macrobond, Mizuho Securities, US Census Bureau

children in 1957. Essentially, most married women became pregnant within seven months of forming a household, and the number of families with three children doubled between 1940 and 1960, while the number of women with four children quadrupled during this period.

Cost-Push Inflation

Organized Labor, the GI Bill, and the Growth of the Middle Class

Just as WWII and the Cold War that followed were a boon for industry, organized labor also benefited. Unions helped spark an explosion in the middle class and the increase in demand associated with the new suburban lifestyle. The critical initial development in these areas that led the growth of the middle class was the "maintenance-of-membership" rule instituted by the National War Labor Board (NWLB). This rule allowed unions to count all new employees as members. The unions could draw dues from all new employee paychecks as long as the employer had already recognized the union. The war effort benefited those industries where unions were already in existence: the large manufacturing companies, steel, shipping, transportation, chemicals, etc. The NWLB also required unionized workplaces in all plants the federal government supported through defense spending. The net effect was an explosion in high-paid union workers. It has been estimated that labor unions expanded to 14.75 million in 1945 from

10.5 million members in 1941, or approximately 35%–36% of the non-agricultural workforce.

To get a sense of how the war effort prompted the growth in the middle class, it is important to recognize the effect it had on high-paying industries. Output in the aircraft industry, for example, increased by over 11-fold between 1940 and 1944, as did shipbuilding. Munitions output expanded by almost 15 times its 1940 production as the output of aluminum more than tripled and rubber doubled. The result was an increase in the level of employment relative to the labor force from almost 13.5% to 98.8% of the labor force over the same four-year period. The unemployment rate dropped from over 14.6% of the labor force to just over 1% in 1944. Not only did the unemployed find jobs—due in large part to the war effort—but the new entrants to the labor force—minorities and women—also found work in high-paying areas. In fact, it is estimated that almost 19 million women were working outside the home by 1945, of which approximately 2 million were employed in war industries.

The new employment opportunities that flowed directly from the war effort, and the explosion of high-paying jobs in new industries during the two decades that followed, increased the number of middle-class households, which in turn added to the excess demand of the postwar period. The tax structure implemented to pay for the war effort also reduced the income inequality that had dominated prior to WWII. National income accounts show that although corporate profits surged during the war, capital income (defined as dividends, interest, rents, and royalties) stagnated as the top corporate tax rate climbed from 20% to more than 50%. The result was higher wages accruing to the top 1% of US households, but a reduction in wage income for the remaining 99%. In fact, studies have shown that anywhere from 40%–45% of national income accrued to the top 1% of households in the period between the two world wars. This measure, however, dropped to about 30% during the war and remained stable in the 31%–32% area until the 1970s, when it began to climb again. By the 1990s, this share of income accruing to the top 1% of households crossed back above 40%.

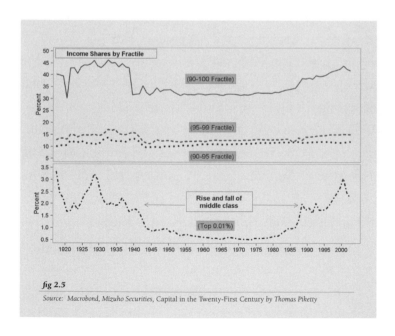

fig 2.5

Source: *Macrobond, Mizuho Securities,* Capital in the Twenty-First Century *by Thomas Piketty*

Great Society

The Great Society experiment of the Kennedy and Johnson years was also partly responsible for the growth of the
middle-class as new labor laws and discriminatory hiring practices were outlawed. In the wake of the Kennedy assassina-
tion in 1963 and the wave of civil unrest sweeping across the
country, the new Johnson administration immediately set out
to implement two previously stalled legislative initiatives. The
Civil Rights Act banned employment discrimination based on
race or gender. Johnson also passed the Economic Opportunity
Act of 1964, which lowered the top marginal tax bracket from
91% to 71%, and lowered the marginal rate in every income
bracket. The tax-cut legislation also lowered corporate taxes.

The Kennedy/Johnson tax cut triggered a postwar prosperity boom. The gross national product (GNP) increased by
7% in 1964, 8% in 1965, and 9% in 1966. Disposable income
rose 15% in 1966. The jobless rate fell below 5% by 1968, and
the average family income doubled what it had been in the late
1950s. The result was a Johnson landslide in the 1964 elec-
tions. The Democratic sweep in the states gave the President
more than a two-thirds majority in each House of the 89th
Congress. The power shift in the Capitol allowed the Johnson administration to pass 84 important pieces of legislation
in its five-plus years. This flurry of legislation was designed
to end poverty, promote equality, rejuvenate cities, and protect the environment. In particular, Johnson's Great Society
experiment authorized Medicare and expanded Medicaid. The
unionized government workforce also expanded to implement

these new programs, which expanded the role of government in the life of ordinary citizens.

Key Johnson Social Initiatives

1. Civil Rights Act of 1964
2. Voting Rights Act of 1965
3. Economic Opportunity Act of 1964
4. Appalachian Regional Development Act of 1965
5. Elementary and Secondary Education Act of 1965
6. Higher Education Act of 1963
7. Higher Education Act of 1965
8. National Defense Education Act of 1964
9. Social Security Act of 1965 (authorized Medicare and expanded Medicaid)
10. Tax Act of 1965 (authorized a 7% increase in Social Security benefits and liberalized disability rules)
11. Social Security Act of 1967 (authorized a 13% increase in old-age, survivor, and disability payments)
12. Food Stamp Act of 1964 (made program permanent)

Environmental and Consumer Safety Awareness

The wave of social consciousness that boiled over into race riots in major cities and into anti-war protests, which dogged the later years of the Johnson administration, expanded the government's role in other areas of the economy. Growing concerns over polluted rivers and streams and deteriorating air quality led to a host of legislation designed to protect the environment. Federal funding for new and improved mass transit was provided. Programs were designed to reduce air and water pollution of factories, mines, and utilities. New agencies and Cabinet-level departments were created to address these issues. Auto emissions rules were initiated, as were auto safety rules. Consumer protection was advanced, and Johnson appointed the first Presidential Assistant for Consumer Affairs. In essence, the Johnson administration, in just a handful of years, permanently altered the government's role in the economy and the social safety net it controlled. This revolution greatly expanded the economy, the government, and the cost of doing business. All of these changes expanded the demand side of the economy while constraining the supply side.

Key Johnson Environmental Initiatives

1. Water Quality Act of 1965
2. Clean Air Act of 1963
3. Wilderness Act of 1964
4. Endangered Species Preservation Act of 1966
5. National Trails Systems Act of 1968
6. Wild and Scenic Rivers Act of 1968
7. Land and Water Conservation Fund Act of 1965
8. Solid Waste Disposal Act of 1965
9. Motor Vehicle Air Pollution Control Act of 1965

10. National Historic Preservation Act of 1966
11. Aircraft Noise Abatement Act of 1968
12. National Environmental Policy Act of 1969

End of the Gold Standard

The social and environmental programs implemented by the Johnson administration stressed the ability of the economy to sustain a low inflation rate as competing demands on fixed resources clashed with the rising cost of doing business in a more regulated environment. The demands created by the Great Society programs and policies added to the growing costs of an increasingly unpopular Vietnam War and those of a rapidly recovering Western Europe and Japan. The result was an upturn in inflation as demand exceeded supply, especially in the short run. The associated decline in real interest rates and real wages exacerbated this situation by stimulating demand. Eventually, organized labor and the providers of loanable funds demanded compensation for the decline in purchasing power, and a wage and price spiral developed. An overvalued dollar resulted in a growing trade deficit in addition to a rising budget deficit. The stress this created on the currency boiled over during the early years of the Nixon administration, and eventually forced the president to end the dollar's convertibility into gold in August 1971. By March 1973, all attempts to revive the fixed exchange rate system of Bretton Woods failed, and the major currencies began to float freely against each other. The associated devaluation of the dollar set the stage for the greatest supply-side shocks of the postwar period and the double-digit inflation of the late 1970s and early 1980s.

THE BRETTON WOODS SYSTEM, PRE-1971

As an Allied victory in Europe became more apparent, the focus among policymakers began to shift toward winning the peace. Allied powers were focused on not making the same mistakes that led to the rise of Nazi Germany and Fascism in Italy so quickly after the end of WWI. Their vision was also shaped by the belief that the flexible exchange rate of the 1930s led to excessive volatility, which damaged the flow of trade. They also concluded that the rigidity of a fixed exchange regime tied to gold was not a viable alternative, given that a substantial portion of global production was in the future Soviet Union.

What emerged from the 730 delegates from all 44 Allied nations that attended the conference in Bretton Woods, New Hampshire, was a "pegged rate" currency regime. Members were required to establish a "parity of their national currency in terms of the reserve currency," the dollar, and to maintain their exchange rates within a 1% band around the peg by intervening in the currency markets. To bolster confidence in the new reserve currency, the dollar was to be convertible into gold at a fixed price of $35 dollars an ounce.

Countries could change their par value by more than 10% relative to the dollar, so long as they received IMF approval. Any country that changed its peg without IMF approval would be denied access to loans from the fund. The IMF was capitalized by its members— initially $8.8 billion made up of 25% in gold or dollars and 75% in the members' own currencies. In the event a member country running a current account deficit should experience payment problems, it could immediately withdraw up to 25% of its quota and could request a foreign currency loan from the fund. These loans needed to be repaid within 18 months to 5 years. Allies also created the International Bank for Reconstruction and Development, to promote world trade and to finance the reconstruction of Europe. It was initially capitalized with $10 billion and was allowed to sell securities to raise additional funds in order to promote economic development.

The strength of the postwar recovery, the growth of West Germany and Japan during the Cold War period, and international dissatisfaction with the Vietnam War all contributed to the eventual demise of the "pegged" exchange rate regime. A surplus of US dollars overseas caused by foreign aid, military spending, and foreign investment by domestic companies left the currency overvalued. Programs designed to stem the flow of dollars overseas by both Presidents Kennedy and Johnson generally failed and led to speculation that the US government would eventually devalue the currency. The result was a wave of dollar selling in the foreign exchange market. The massive run on the dollar in 1971 led President Nixon to announce a temporary suspension of the dollar's convertibility into gold. This was intended to provide a transition period in which the dollar could be devalued to a new, more sustainable level. After months of negotiations, the G-10 established a new set of fixed exchange rates, and by December 1971, the Smithsonian Agreement devalued the dollar from $35 per ounce of gold to $38, but convertibility was not reintroduced. By February 1973 the dollar was again devalued to $42 an ounce. Just one month later, however, the dollar was again under intense downward pressure and the G-10

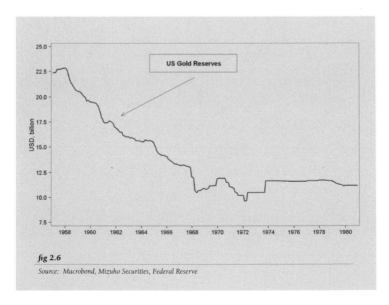

fig 2.6

Source: *Macrobond, Mizuho Securities, Federal Reserve*

approved a new program wherein the six members of the European Union tied their currencies together and jointly floated them against the dollar. There is no doubt that the October 1973 oil embargo was at least partially the result of the fact that oil was denominated in dollars just as the currency was under intense downward pressure.

Supply Shocks and the Great Inflation

Environmental activism and the social consciousness of the 1960s started to increase the cost of doing business for domestic companies, as the cost of compliance grew rapidly and surging global demand pulled up inflation. The desire to reduce carbon emissions also led to an increased dependence on oil relative to cheaper coal. The decline in petroleum production underway in a number of the world's top producers, which began in the 1960s, made the situation worse. Germany reached peak production in 1966, Venezuela and the United States in 1970, and Iran in 1974. Inflation pressures building in the wake of a strong global economy also helped weaken the dollar's link to gold, and, when it finally broke in 1973, the pressures on dollar-based commodities and their producers increased sharply.

Union power was also reaching its peak around this time, as labor sought to retain the standard of living achieved in the first 15–20 years after the war when inflation began to eat away at household purchasing power. Important geopolitical developments were also taking place in the Middle East; these would have a profound effect on both energy politics and markets. This confluence of factors created the perfect storms of demand-pull and cost-push inflation.

1973 Oil Crisis

On October 16, 1973, just days into the Yom Kippur War between Israel, Egypt, and Syria, and in response to President Nixon's request for $2.2 billion in emergency aid for Israel to resupply its military, the Organization of Arab Petroleum Exporting Countries (OAPEC) announced a sharp increase in the posted price of oil. This decision was quickly followed by an all-out embargo against the United States. The unanticipated military conflict was initiated to retake the land lost to Israel during the June 1967 Six-Day War. The embargo was also targeted against Canada, Japan, the Netherlands, and the UK. OAPEC used the embargo to create a rift among NATO members in order to maximize the pressure on the US for its support of Israel. The embargo lasted until March 1974 and only ended after an agreement was reached in which Israel would pull back to the east side of the Suez Canal.

The hike in crude oil prices was not just in response to

the geopolitical conflict with Israel. The oil-producing nations were also being squeezed by a depreciating dollar and the price hikes undertaken by Western suppliers of wheat, sugar, cement, and refined products being sold in exchange for the petro dollars earned. Attempts by OAPEC to change the benchmark for oil from the dollar to gold had also failed prior to the embargo. Initially, the posted price of crude oil was raised 70% to $5.11 per barrel; and to boost the effectiveness of the hike, the members of OAPEC agreed to an immediate 5% production cut. Additional reductions in increments of 5% were also planned until their economic and political objectives were met. By October 20, 1973, frustrations among the Arab producers boiled over, and Libya announced a blockade of all deliveries to the US, which was quickly followed by other nations, including Saudi Arabia. The inelastic short-run

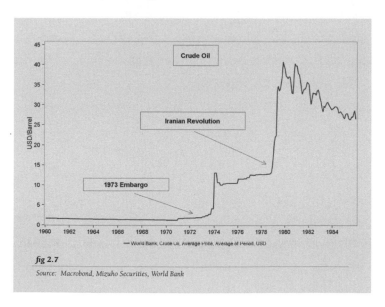

fig 2.7

Source: *Macrobond, Mizuho Securities, World Bank*

demand for oil pushed the price of crude up from $3 per barrel to $12 per barrel before a reduction in demand established a new temporary equilibrium.

The spike in the price of crude oil caused significant disruptions to the domestic and global economy, which eventually pushed supply and demand back into better balance—though at a much higher price.

But the quadrupling of the price was also the result of ill-conceived price controls imposed by the Nixon administration. The system limited the price of previously discovered "old oil" while allowing newly discovered oil to be sold at a higher price to encourage exploration. This tended to keep old oil off the market, leading to a system of rationing to address the associated disruption in supply. By the last week of February 1974 the misallocation of oil and refined products had created an environment in which an estimated 20% of gas stations had no fuel. The increased cost of energy resulted in a combination of increased conservation and exploration; this eventually stabilized prices.

Iranian Revolution

Crude oil prices drifted steadily upward for about five years after the lifting of the embargo. The price of crude rose to $15 per barrel from about $10 per barrel before spiking dramatically higher in 1979. A combination of geopolitical forces and a general weakening in the currency contributed to the sharp rise in imported crude oil prices that occurred as the decade drew to a close. In the wake of the Iranian Revolution and the fall of the US-supported Shah, the country's production of crude oil crashed. Saudi Arabia and other OPEC countries increased production; but overall, output still declined by about 4%. Although the decline in production was relatively moderate, the reaction in the crude oil market was dramatic. The Carter administration's inability to deal with the taking of US Embassy personnel in Tehran as hostages of the revolution increased the supply paranoia that gripped the oil market. Growing tensions between Iraq and Iran for dominance in the region kept supply tensions high. The Sunni government of Saddam Hussein feared the religious revolution led by Ayatollah Khomeini in Iran would spread to Iraq's suppressed Shia population. These tensions boiled over, and in September 1980, when Iraq launched an attack on Iran, the conflict destroyed Iran's oil production capabilities. The result was a cumulative spike in crude oil to $40 per barrel from $15.

The negative macro effects stemming from this rise in the price of crude oil would prove to be a game-changer for policy-makers and central bankers in the industrialized economies as a wage-price spiral became well established. The acute domestic inflation dynamic created significant downward pressure on the exchange value of the dollar, and inflation seemed completely out of control in the late 1970s and early 1980s. Inflation began to dominate the domestic political dialogue as well as household behavior and corporate decision making. The result was a dramatic shift in the course of both fiscal and monetary policy, even though the spike in crude oil prices led to a rapid shift away from oil toward cheaper natural gas and other alternative energy sources.

Conservation efforts were expanded dramatically at the individual, corporate, and government levels. A struggle for market share ensued among the OAPEC producers as exploration of previously uneconomical oil fields increased the available supply, which then led to an oil glut by the mid-1980s and a plunge in prices.

However, the macroeconomic forces unleashed by the Great Inflation and the policies implemented to bring prices back under control triggered a chain of events that would transit the economy from excess demand to excess supply—the situation plaguing the domestic and global economy today. This shift also changed the very nature of the business cycle. Instead of being driven by cyclical inflation dynamics, the three recessions experienced since the late 1980s have been caused by developments in the credit markets.

A DEEP AND LONG RECESSION

The 1970s was a period of limited economic growth, and the rapidly rising price of crude oil was clearly a major contributor. The increase in energy prices not only added to inflation and created a world of rising inflation expectations, but it also added to the cost of producing goods and services. Perhaps the most damaging effect was the increased obsolescence of capital goods. Domestic manufacturing was designed to run on cheap energy. A quadrupling of the price of energy early in the decade, followed by an even more dramatic price hike in the wake of the Iranian Revolution and the Iran–Iraq War, left many companies with outdated, inefficient technology. The associated collapse in earnings and the rising cost of debt financing limited the ability of domestic manufacturers to quickly replace inefficient capital stock with new, more reliable, and more efficient machinery.

The S&P 500 declined by 48.2% between September 1973 and March 1975, making equity financing difficult. Short-term interest rates rose to a peak of 10.92% in September 1973 from 3.45% in February 1972, as long-term interest rates rose by over 150 basis points to their cyclical peak. According to the National Bureau of Economic Research (NBER), the economy fell into a deep recession in November 1973 and did not begin to recover until March 1975. Specifically, the economy contracted by 3.3% in the first quarter (1Q) of 1974, as oil prices spiked and contracted another 9% cumulatively over the next four quarters, even though crude oil prices stabilized.

The decline in real GDP during the 1973–1975 recession was dominated by a collapse in investment spending as industrial production tumbled by 13.1% over the 16 months—from peak to trough—of the recession. In addition to the length and depth of this recession relative to the five prior postwar downturns, the most important aspect of the spike in crude oil prices was the dampening effect it appears to have had on a number of key economic metrics over the balance of the decade. Output growth in the 1971–1979 period was about one-third of that experienced during the 1960–1973 period.

Labor productivity also slumped in the 1973–1979 period. Output per hour slowed to just 1.2% from 3.3%, even as the number of hours worked declined. The result was a period of rapidly rising inflation, which would eventually lead to an inflation rate approaching 15%. This set in motion powerful forces that shifted the world from a state of excess demand to that of excess supply, and changed the nature of business cycles from inflation to credit cycles.

Politics and the Shift from Demand- to Supply-Focused Policies

"Morning Again in America"

This quote from President Reagan's second inaugural address best conveys the transition in the US economy that took place during his first term in office. The US economy and America's place in the world emerged from the darkness of stagflation and foreign policy vacillation into a world of growth and international ascendance. The Reagan revolution reflected a break with conventional Keynesian macro policies in favor of the laissez-faire philosophy advanced by Milton Friedman. The result was a sharp reversal in the direction of the economy. The guiding principle underlying the Reagan economic policy was succinctly stated in his first inaugural address when he asserted that the "government is not the solution to our problems: Government is the problem." The shift in tone coming out of Washington was much broader than that expressed by a mere economic ideologue, and it became apparent on day one.

As the newly sworn-in president was delivering his address on the Capitol steps, Iran released 52 American hostages who had been held at the US Embassy compound in Tehran for the last 444 days of the Carter administration.

President Reagan would question the orthodox policies that had guided the intellectual debates and policies inside and outside the beltway as well as in foreign affairs during his tenure. In addition to cutting taxes and increasing defense spending, he cut regulation and showed that the union grip on the labor markets could be successfully challenged. His unflappable optimism and "get-it-done" mentality was just the medicine the electorate and corporate America needed, and he was willing to spend money to get things done. The results began to materialize quickly. During Reagan's administration, the civilian jobless rate declined to just 5.4% from an average of 7.5% under President Carter. However, the unemployment rate peaked at 10.8% in 1982 and 10.4% in 1984. Real GDP grew at an average of 3.4% during Reagan's eight years in office, with a peak growth rate of 8.6% in 1983. Inflation also fell to 4.4% from 12.5% during his last year in office. The Reagan approach of stimulating the supply side of the economy through tax cuts and deregulation while supporting the Fed's anti-inflation monetary policy had a profound effect on the domestic economy. The unintended consequences of his hardline stance on the air traffic controllers' strike also served as a powerful force behind the economic transition from excess demand to excess supply and from inflation to credit cycles.

In foreign policy, Reagan sensed a change in the Soviet

leadership under Mikhail Gorbachev, and he pivoted from escalating the arms race in his first term to diplomacy in his later term. The Saudi Arabian market share grab in 1985 cut crude oil prices by two-thirds and severely reduced Russia's ability to fund its economy and military spending, leading to a greater willingness to negotiate reductions in nuclear and conventional weapons. The two world leaders would sign the Intermediate-Range Nuclear Force Treaty (INF), which eliminated an entire class of nuclear weapons. They also laid the groundwork for the Strategic Arms Reduction Treaty, or START, initiative. In a famous speech at the Berlin Wall in 1987, Reagan called on Gorbachev to "tear down this wall." In November 1989, ten months after Reagan left office, the Berlin Wall fell and the Cold War came to a close. As support from the USSR waned, the East German government collapsed, leading to German reunification and eventually to the European Monetary Union (EMU).

Trickle-Down Economics

The guiding principles behind "Reaganomics" were that lower tax rates would stimulate the supply side of the economy enough to expand the tax base and more than offset the loss in tax revenue from households and/or corporate taxpayers. This supply-side expansion was championed by economist Arthur Laffer, and it formed the basis of the new administration's first budget program. His "peace through strength" foreign policy initiative was also a key part of his first budget and led to the largest peacetime increase in defense spending in history.

The Economic Recovery Tax Act (ERTA), or the Kemp–Roth tax cut, was enacted in 1981. This legislation included an across-the-board reduction in marginal tax rates. The cumulative effect of the law was a 25% reduction in tax rates over a three-year phase-in period. The top tax rate was cut from 70% to 50% while the bottom tax rate was dropped from 14% to 11%. In addition, the new tax brackets were indexed to inflation, with the implementation delayed until 1985. ERTA also created a 10% exclusion on income for two-wage-earner families, in essence eliminating the marriage penalty. The estate tax exemption was also increased in steps to $600,000 from $175,625 in 1987. All working taxpayers were allowed to establish an IRA, and ERTA also expanded provisions for

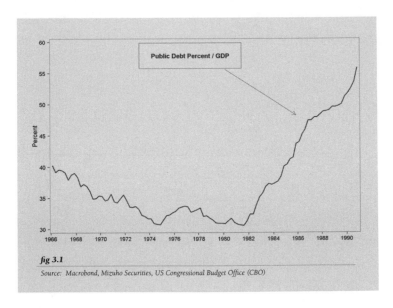

fig 3.1

Source: Macrobond, Mizuho Securities, US Congressional Budget Office (CBO)

employee stock ownership plans. The $200 interest exclusion was replaced with 15% net interest exclusion up to a $900 cap, beginning in 1985. Corporate taxes were cut $150 billion over five years through accelerated depreciation and a reduced windfall profits tax.

Following on the heels of the Kemp–Roth tax cut, Congress passed and the president signed a tax hike of some kind in every year from 1981 to 1987, and yet the economy surged. The expanding economy created an estimated 16 million new jobs, and the tax cut has been seen as a model for all conservative politicians since. Although federal tax receipts rose by an average of 8.2% per year between 1980 and 1989, federal outlays rose by 7.1%, resulting in a surge in the budget deficit to $152.1 billion in FY89 from $73 billion in FY80, and a peak deficit of $221.2 billion. The cumulative effect of the spike in the deficit was more than a threefold increase in the public debt outstanding to $2.8 trillion, or almost a 50% increase in debt to GDP during the president's two terms. Statistically, it has never been conclusively shown that the Reagan deficits increased real yields, but the dramatic rise in the exchange value of the dollar and the decline in long-term rates in the wake of the Clinton tax hike of 1993 clearly suggest the deficit was a major factor.

Deregulation was also a key component of Reaganomics and/or the supply-side revolution. The idea was simply to reduce red tape and get the government out of the way of business so that companies could grow again. Specifically, the Reagan team moved quickly to eliminate the Nixon-era price

controls on oil and natural gas, and the result was a rapid easing of supply shortages that had plagued the economy and
eventually produced lower energy prices. He eased regulation
on cable TV, long-distance telephone service, interstate bus
service, and shipping. The biggest critics of his deregulation
efforts cite the bank regulations that were eased in 1982 and
suggest deregulation eventually caused the savings and loan
(S&L) crisis. The Garn–St. Germain Depository Institution Act
removed loan-to-value restrictions on S&Ls, and by reducing
regulatory staff at the Federal Home Loan Bank Board, banks
were indirectly allowed to increase their involvement in riskier real estate ventures. It is interesting that the thrift crises in
the 1990s would create the first postwar business cycle that
was the result of a credit and not an inflation problem in the
economy.

The Kemp–Roth tax cut and deregulation were viewed by
the president and his advisors as key to expanding the supply side of the economy in order to end stagflation—or an
environment in which both inflation and unemployment rose
simultaneously. But it would be his push for free trade and the
way he handled the air traffic controllers' strike that would
have the greatest effect on stimulating the supply side of the
economy in subsequent years. President Reagan promoted
free trade by launching the Uruguay Round in 1986, which
eventually lowered global trade barriers and created the World
Trade Organization (WTO).

He also started the push for the North America Free
Trade Agreement (NAFTA). However, import trade barriers

were actually raised during his administration. The voluntary import restraint on cars and light trucks from Japan was a clear example of how the rising dollar increased import competition, and the politics of job creation led to a two-track trade agenda under his administration.

The clash between the tight monetary policy imposed by the Volcker Fed and the president's simulative fiscal policy resulted in an overvalued currency, a surging budget deficit, and a hollowing out of the American manufacturing industry. The political pressure confronting Reagan's free trade agenda led to a virtual doubling of the number of imported items subject to some form of restraint, but the free trade seeds he sowed took root and the expansion of trade policies under George H.W. Bush and Bill Clinton would play an important role in transitioning to excess supply. In fact, the NAFTA

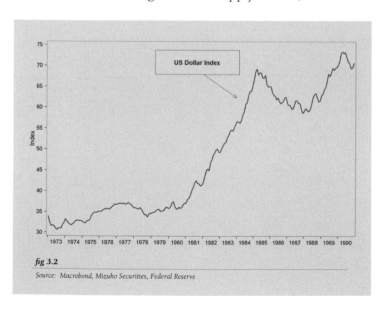

fig 3.2

Source: *Macrobond, Mizuho Securities, Federal Reserve*

agreement was negotiated and signed by President Bush and was approved by Congress under President Clinton in 1992.

The Professional Air Traffic Controllers Organization (PATCO) conducted an illegal strike in 1981, seeking better working conditions, a pay raise, and a 32-hour workweek. President Reagan was quick to respond and ordered the strikers back to work, declaring that the work stoppage was a "peril to national safety." When the striking workers refused to return to work, the president fired all controllers who did not return to work. This show of resolve and longer-term focus sold well domestically and internationally, and, as a result, there were no further illegal work stoppages. By contrast, between 1962 and 1981 there had been 39 illegal strikes by federal employees.

Most labor economists see the decision to fire the controllers as the beginning of the end for organized labor, which

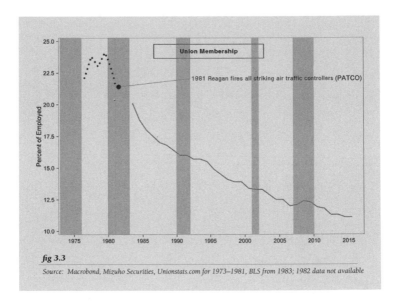

fig 3.3

Source: Macrobond, Mizuho Securities, Unionstats.com for 1973–1981, BLS from 1983; 1982 data not available

was already under stress as a result of increased international competition. In retrospect, it is clear today that the air traffic controllers' strike and President Reagan's handling of this labor dispute probably had a greater long-term effect on the economy than any of his other economic decisions—other than the push for free trade. As a former president of the Screen Actors Guild and a champion of collective bargaining, the decision to fire the air traffic controllers unintentionally shifted the balance of power in favor of management, and the result is today's highly flexible labor market environment. The loss in power and prestige suffered by labor unions not only added to the growing income inequality in the economy, it also helped to accelerate the rise in institutional and globalized wealth that provided the financial support for the expansion in the supply side of the economy.

Al Gore: "I Invented the Internet!"

The above misquote is one of the most famous things that never actually happened. Vice President Gore instead asserted, "I took initiative in creating the Internet" during an interview with Wolf Blitzer of CNN. Although this was a true statement, it was an unfortunate choice of words.

The vice president's support for legislation that aided in the development of the Internet cannot be denied. As a congressman, a senator, and later as vice president, Al Gore was a major supporter of technology. In fact, he crafted the High Performance Computing and Communication Act of 1991. This Act, commonly referred to as "The Gore Bill," was signed into law by President Bush in December 1991, and provided $600 million in funding for high-performance computing. The bill brought together industry, academia, and the government to develop and deploy gigabit/sec networking. Gore's legislation helped fund the programmers at the University of Illinois who created the first Web browser. Mosaic was released in 1993 and is generally considered the beginning of the Internet boom. In the fall of 1990 there were only 313,000 computers connected to the Internet; but by 1996, there were close to 10 million.

Networking and its implications became a hot topic during the 1992 Clinton–Gore election campaign, and after being sworn in, the new administration set in place a number of initiatives for a national information infrastructure aimed at ensuring that all Americans would be able to access the Web. Although the Clinton team saw this new technology as a source of new, high-paying jobs, which it was and still is, they did not foresee the larger, longer-term ramifications. Companies such as Amazon, Google, and PayPal experienced such rapid growth that more traditional companies had to focus aggressively on cutting costs to compete in the equity market. These new technology- and Internet-based companies increased competition; and, although the consumers liked the lower prices they paid for goods, wages suffered. The information superhighway has

had a major negative macro effect on the balance between supply and demand, both domestically and internationally.

Investing in Science and Technology

The Clinton–Gore team increased funding for civilian research
and development by 43% but did not cut defense research.
They also increased R&D spending to universities by 53%.
Between 1993 and 2000, President Clinton invested an additional $10 billion in a range of science and technology pro-
grams included in the 21st Century Research Fund, which
helped fund the next generation's scientists and engineers.
The administration also supported technology through legislation. In 1998, the president signed the Internet Tax Free-
dom Act, which bars federal, state, and local governments
from taxing Internet access and from imposing discriminatory
Internet-only taxes. He also signed the Digital Millennium
Copyright Act, which increased intellectual property protection. In June 2000, President Clinton signed the Electronic
Signatures in Global and National Commerce Act, which gave
online contracts the same force of law as paper contracts.
The most important initiatives that fostered the growth of
the Internet, however, were the economic programs implemented by the Clinton administration, and the strong economy that followed.

The Clinton strategy of fiscal discipline, open foreign markets, and investment in the future produced a record 120 months of expansion. Real GDP averaged 4% per year, and 22 million jobs were created, of which 97% were in the private sector. The decline in interest rates that followed the implementation of the first Clinton budget helped increase home ownership from 64.2% of households to a record high of 67.7%. Joblessness fell from more than 7% in 1993 to a mere 4% by the end of 2000, the lowest level in more than 40 years. The housing and equity market booms that resulted further cultivated the perception that double-digit investment returns were achievable over the long term and that the economic transition from a manufacturing-based to an information-based economy would eliminate the business cycle altogether. While the Clinton expansion was powered by declining long-term

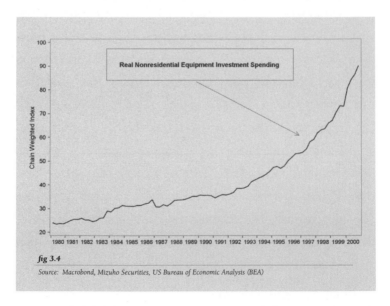

fig 3.4

Source: Macrobond, Mizuho Securities, US Bureau of Economic Analysis (BEA)

rates, the accommodative monetary policy of Fed Chairman Alan Greenspan also contributed to the expansion of the supply side of the economy. Record corporate investment led to the false conclusion that a virtuous cycle of investment—leading to increased employment and wealth generation—was self-sustaining. Instead, the result was excessive investment in labor-saving technologies.

The capital deepening boosted productivity, while the free flow of goods in North America spilled over into other regions as companies sought alternative, lower-cost sources for goods in order to drive up profits. Managing for shareholder value (greater returns) forced more traditional companies to compete with information-oriented growth companies on a return basis. The result was a significant expansion in the economy's ability to produce both goods and services as capital was substituted for labor. Essentially, the decline in long-term rates that eluded both Reagan and Bush occurred under Clinton and fostered an expansion in the supply side of the economy that outstripped the increase in demand. This dampened inflation and left the business cycle to be determined by credit quality developments. Flexible labor market policies also kept inflation under control, and the bipartisan desire to "end welfare" added another key driver behind the shift to excess supply.

The key labor market contribution made by the Clinton White House was signing the Personal Responsibility and Work Opportunity Act in August 1996. This legislation was designed to increase labor market participation among public assistance recipients. This was accomplished by ending welfare as an entitlement and imposing a five-year lifetime cap on benefits. The result was an infusion of workers during the latter stages of the "baby bust" years, which dampened wages, boosted profits, and increased investment spending.

Unfortunately, the cracks in the virtuous cycle started to show through, and in March 2000, the NASDAQ peaked at 5,132.52 and then plunged to a low of 1,114.1 on October 9, 2002. The housing bubble, on the other hand, continued to build through the George W. Bush years as speculation driven by wealth creation, bank accommodation, and Fannie Mae balance sheet expansion supported the market. This second Clinton-inspired credit bubble did not burst until December 2007.

Key Aspects of the Clinton/GOP Welfare Legislation

- Required welfare recipients to begin working after two years of receiving benefits
- Placed a lifetime limit of five years on benefits paid by federal funds
- Provided incentives to two-parent families and discouraged out-of-wedlock births
- Enhanced enforcement of child-support agreements
- Required state and professional licenses to be withheld from illegal immigrants
- Granted states wider latitude in designing their welfare programs

The Omnibus Budget Reconciliation Act of 1993, or unofficially, the Deficit Reduction Act of 1993, built on the "pay as you go" policy enacted by President George H.W. Bush and set the stage for a dramatic decline in real long-term interest rates. The new president's fiscal policy lowered long-term mortgage rates, and Franklin Raines, CEO of FNMA, expanded the role of government-sponsored enterprises, or GSEs, in order to increase affordability to what he called underserved families. In 1994 he launched a $1 trillion financing initiative to help fund home ownership for 10 million households, and in 2000 he pledged another $2 trillion to help another 18 million households obtain mortgages.

The first Clinton budget focused on balancing the budget rather than on middle-class tax cuts, just as the Republicans in Congress advocated. His treasury secretary, Robert Rubin (formerly of Goldman Sachs), and his budget coordinator, Roger Altman (founder of a boutique M&A investment bank), led the push for higher taxes in order to lower long-term rates. The budget bill raised taxes on the wealthiest 1.2% of taxpayers while cutting taxes for 15 million low-income households. The tax hike on the wealthy was accomplished by creating two new tax brackets of 36% on income above $115,000 and 39.5% for incomes over $250,000. The people in the $250,000 and above bracket were referred to as millionaires by the White House. A top bracket of 31% had previously been applied to all incomes over $51,900. The earned income tax credit was generously increased and adjusted for inflation in order to reduce taxes on the working poor and to encourage work over welfare. The $135,000 income cap on the 2.9% Medicare tax was eliminated, while a tax of 4.3 cents per gallon was imposed on transportation fuels. The 24% alternative minimum tax rate was raised to a tiered 26% and 28%. The Deficit Reduction Act created new tax brackets of 35% for companies earning $10–$15 million, 38% for earnings of $15–$18.33 million, and 35% for companies generating more than $18.33 million.

The aggressive nature of the Clinton tax hike ran directly into unified Republican opposition to the bill. In the House of Representatives, the bill passed with not one vote being cast for the tax hike from the other side of the aisle; in the Senate, the bill passed only after the vice president cast the deciding vote. The result was a narrowing deficit in every year through 1998 and the first surplus since 1969. The surplus peaked at $236.2 billion in fiscal 2000 before starting to reverse in the following year. The 1998–2001 surpluses reduced to public debt outstanding, but the growing balance in the Social Security trust funds meant that the total public debt increased every year of the Clinton administration.

The seeds of the supply-side revolution sown under President Reagan finally took root under President Clinton. This 20-year period experienced an expansion in the length of business cycle upturns and a general easing of inflation. The dark days of stagflation had been replaced by optimism, increased global trade, the ascendancy of capitalism, and the birth of a new industry—tech—that promised to change the world more dramatically than had the Industrial Revolution in the late 1700s and early 1800s. The technology we all take for granted these days was the stuff of science fiction and spy novels when President Reagan took office, but had become mainstream by the time the Clintons left 1600 Pennsylvania Avenue in 2001.

Quantifying the economic effect of digital technology in almost every aspect of our daily lives is practically impossible, but a few have tried to assess the effect of commercializing the Web—and the numbers are staggering. One study, in fact, suggests that each Internet-related job supports approximately 1.54 jobs elsewhere in the economy, or roughly 2% of the employed workforce. The advertising-supported Internet creates an estimated annual value of $444 billion. About 190 million Americans spend, on average, 68 hours a month on the Internet. A conservative valuation of this time is an

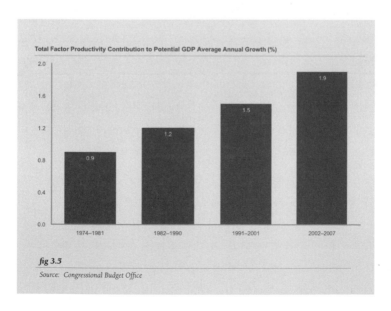

fig 3.5

Source: *Congressional Budget Office*

estimated $680 billion. The acceleration in corporate invest-ment spending that was associated with the explosion of the Internet significantly expanded the economy's ability to pro-duce goods and services. According to the Congressional Bud-get Office (CBO), potential total factor productivity dipped to just 0.9% between 1974 and 1981, but accelerated steadily though the Reagan–Clinton years, and peaked at about 1.9% between 2002 and 2007.

This expansion in the supply side of the economy con-tributed significantly to the transition from excess demand to excess supply, which not only extended the life of business cycle upturns but also changed the nature of the business cycle from being driven by inflation to being a derivative of changing credit quality in the economy. Specifically, the three economic contractions experienced since 1990 have been caused by credit-related developments: the collapse of the thrift indus-try, the collapse of the commercial paper market, and, most recently, the collapse of the household balance sheet. These credit-driven cycles contrast with the inflation cycles of the postwar period up to the 1990s, not only in their cause, but also in the shallow nature of the associated recoveries.

The Final Straw

The supply-side revolution that began under Reagan and Clin-ton found a second wind in the emergence of China from its agrarian roots to being the manufacturing powerhouse it is today. China's influence on the world economy exploded after it joined the World Trade Organization (WTO) in December 2001. The effect of China's growth on the global excess supply situation became even more pronounced in 2008 when, under the leadership of President Hu Jintao, the Chinese government launched an RMB 4 trillion (US $568 billion) fiscal stimulus program along with an aggressive easing of monetary policy. China's government wanted to minimize the negative effects of the global financial crisis on the local economy and show the world their economic structure was superior to the West's unbridled capitalism.

The stimulus program was large enough to add 0.7% to the World Bank's estimate of China's 2009 growth forecast. The problem for the global economy was that even though China avoided most of the adverse effects of the crisis, the

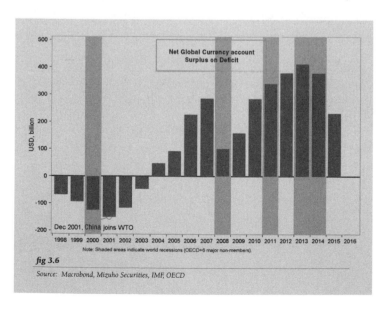

fig 3.6

Source: *Macrobond, Mizuho Securities, IMF, OECD*

added investment compounded the excess supply situation in tradable goods. It also prompted additional investment in the production of raw materials required to feed the Chinese economy under the unrealistic assumption that China would continue to deliver double-digit growth. Unfortunately, the short-term benefits of the 2008 stimulus were overwhelmed by the long-term cost of a surge in debt owed, especially by local governments and state-owned enterprises. The resulting debt hangover has resulted in a loss of economic momentum in China that looks to be structural rather than transitory.

This downshift in growth has exacerbated the global excess supply situation. Excess supply has limited corporate pricing power, squeezed margins, left Japan struggling to exit deflation, pushed Europe into what appears to be a debt/deflation trap, and left China struggling with wholesale deflation pressures. Our own economy is confronting these very same forces and continues to struggle to maintain trend growth. If it were not for our large service industry, we would probably be experiencing our own deflation problem.

CHINA'S RAPID RISE

China has gone from a poor agrarian economy to an industrial powerhouse in just 35 years. An argument can be made that this is an even more important economic development than the digital revolution that has touched every aspect of our lives. The combination of these two events makes the Industrial

Revolution look tiny by comparison. The reason the Chinese transformation is so important is because less than 10% of the world is currently fully industrialized; and if China can successfully make the leap beyond the middle-income level, then an additional 20% of the world's population will enter the modern age. China's growth is spilling over into other areas across Asia, Latin America, Africa, and even in the industrialized West. Let's put China's rapid rise in perspective.

Thirty-five years ago, in 1980, China's per capita income was only one-third that of sub-Saharan Africa. Today China produces roughly 50% of the world's manufactured goods. This includes steel, cement, new vehicles, high-speed trains, robots, ships, machine tools, and cell phones. It also produces 150% more industrial patent application than we do domestically. China overtook the US as the largest manufacturing base in the world in 2010. China is also the largest infrastructure developer, building more tunnels, bridges, and highways than any other nation. As a comparison, China now accounts for approximately 17% of global GDP, up from just 2.4% in 1980; meanwhile, the US economy has slid from 22% to about 16%.

This rapid expansion has led to speculation that China's rapid growth is nothing more than a gigantic government-engineered bubble. Remember, this is not the first time China has attempted to industrialize. In fact, history shows that China has failed three times before. However, the current model being followed is uniquely Chinese; they are not attempting to emulate the Japanese, American, or Soviet models. The current plan is based loosely on the British development model by steadily moving up the development ladder from proto-regional industrial development. However, the government has used its authority to make sure political stability is never threatened by development. Although the question of sustainability cannot be ignored, China's contribution to the world of excess supply cannot be denied.

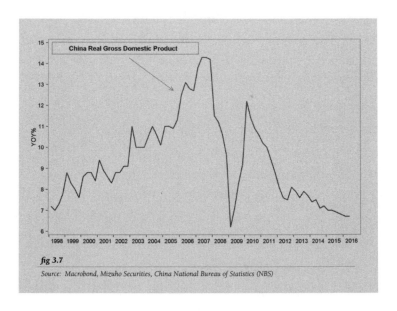

fig 3.7

Source: Macrobond, Mizuho Securities, China National Bureau of Statistics (NBS)

The Great Inflation

Causes

Economists refer to the period from 1965 to 1980 as the Great Inflation. During this 15-year period, headline inflation—the All Items Consumer Price Index—rose to 10.5% in March 1980 from just 1.1% in January 1965. Economists have been fascinated by this period almost to the same extent as they are drawn to the period of the Great Depression. Many of the analyses of this period tend to center on the causes of this abrupt acceleration in prices and on the negative macroeconomic consequences brought about by rapidly rising prices. Central bankers' contributions to both the acceleration in inflation and its more recent downturn dominate another area of research.

Our interest in the Great Inflation is directed more toward the events it triggered and how they helped shape the world of excess supply we live in today. In particular, the institutionalization and globalization of wealth and the belief that double-digit returns are the norm—not the exception—are critical developments of policies implemented to reverse the acceleration in inflation during this period. The interaction between these three developments set the stage for the transition from excess demand to excess supply. This fundamental shift has dominated economic developments and the business cycle since the late 1980s. However, members of the economic community continue to view the world as dominated by excess demand, ignoring the critical transition that is at the heart of today's macroeconomic problem—global deflation rates.

The policy response to the Great Inflation triggered the fundamental changes in the economy that explain why inflation cycles have given way to credit cycles in the wake of the move from excess demand to excess supply. As such, an understanding of how policymakers initially misread the early

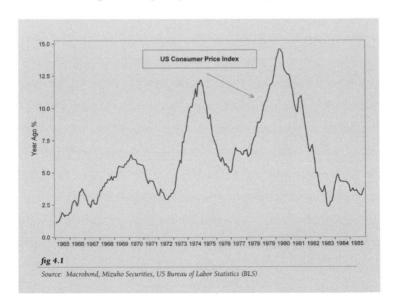

fig 4.1

Source: *Macrobond, Mizuho Securities, US Bureau of Labor Statistics (BLS)*

signs of building inflation pressures in the late 1950s and early 1960s can also provide insight into why deflationary pressures have been largely ignored since the 1990s. For over 25 years, the changed nature of the business cycle has been largely overlooked, even though the last three business cycles have been associated with major credit events—not with demand-led inflation.

There are two paths of analysis economists tend to explore when studying the acceleration in inflation from 1965–1980. First, economists tend to highlight the major fundamental changes in the domestic and global economy that corresponded with the general rise in prices. Second, they tend to look at the policy mistakes made by the Fed during this period. Although most mainstream economists tend to see the latter explanation—Fed errors—as the most compelling explanation for why inflation seemed to have gone out of control, this is somewhat self-serving. To lay the blame solely at the feet of the Federal Reserve allows the economic community to take credit for the disinflationary period that followed in the wake of the decisive anti-inflation policies that had been implemented by Fed Chairman Paul Volcker in the early 1980s, and then followed religiously by his predecessors.

By contrast, my heuristic approach suggests that the Fed's anti-inflationary policies triggered a series of fundamental changes in the economy that led us from one unsustainable path to a potentially more destructive alternative path, a debt/deflation feedback loop.

The major fundamental changes in the economy following

the Great Depression and WWII were discussed in great detail in the previous chapter. However, a quick summary of these considerations will be useful for pulling together the different threads that led, as one cohesive dynamic, to the Great Inflation. Following this discussion, a look at the policy mistakes made during this period of rising inflation will close the loop on the inflationary forces that altered global economic balances and set the stage for today's deflationary risks.

The end of WWII left the world economy in shambles, but it offered great opportunity for the victors—especially the United States. As a new superpower with its military, security, and economic interests spread around the globe, the US economy flourished. Unlike most other participants in the war, the US domestic manufacturing base not only survived the conflict, but it emerged from the fighting significantly expanded

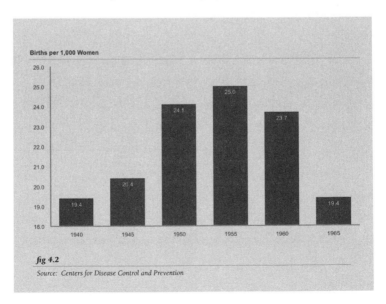

fig 4.2

Source: *Centers for Disease Control and Prevention*

and more productive. The increased opportunities in overseas markets and the new monetary system centered on the dollar meant that both corporate America and its workers were able to benefit simultaneously from the new prosperity. The result was a powerful combination of a rising domestic and global demand for US-made products. This demand-led economy pulled up wages, raised the standard of living, and sparked a population boom as returning veterans rushed to make up for lost time.

The middle-class dream suddenly became attainable. The security demands of being the leader of the free world also resulted in the development of a large, permanent military industrial complex, and the Cold War inspired a push for new technology to secure peace and expand horizons into outer space. These developments were supported by government policies that extended the boom well into the 1960s. The optimism inspired by this "anything is possible" mentality led to Johnson's Great Society reforms and the Kennedy-inspired tax cut. These developments pushed the economy further forward, even as the postwar boom was beginning to fade.

The demand-induced inflationary pressures eventually led to the collapse of the postwar monetary system, which was loosely anchored to gold. In its wake, this development sowed the seeds of the Great Inflation. The increased costs associated with President Johnson's social, environmental, and regulatory reforms contributed to a wage-price spiral that was exacerbated by the postwar power of unions. Union organizers used strikes, rulebook slowdowns, and collective bargaining to preserve the gains made by their workers in the 1950s. A series of oil price shocks and food price increases added a cost-push element to inflationary pressures in the domestic and global economies.

Complicating matters was the steadfast adherence by the economics community and policymakers of the time to an orthodox version of Keynesian stabilization policies. Memory of the unprecedented unemployment of the 1930s and the explanation for the Depression offered by Keynes led to an inherent bias among policymakers to use the tools they controlled to accommodate expansionary fiscal policy actions. This coordinated approach was codified in the Employment Act of 1946. Among other things, the Act specified that it was the responsibility of the federal government "to promote maximum employment, production, and purchasing power," and provide for greater coordination between fiscal and monetary policy to achieve this end. The 1946 Act is the underlying basis for the 1978 Humphrey–Hawkins Act and the Fed's current dual mandate to promote maximum employment and stable prices. The critical assumption policymakers made in the 1960s and 1970s that contributed to the acceleration in inflation was that there was a long-term exploitable trade-off between unemployment and inflation, known as the Phillips curve.

The new large-scale computer-based econometric model used at that time to assess the effect of alternative fiscal and monetary policy paths assumed that the potential employment gains from simulative policies were substantially greater than the cost associated with the anticipated small rise in prices. Unfortunately, the Phillips curve proved to be anything but stable. Critics of the policies being advanced at the time suggested that once people began to expect prices to keep rising, the Phillips curve would shift upward; as a result, it would generate substantially more inflation than the models of the day were projecting. Some of the critics of these policies suggested that the Phillips curve relationship was vertical in the long run. The historical data support their claims that virtually no long-term gains in employment would be achieved and that higher inflation is all that these policies would produce.

The principal result from trying to exploit the Phillips curve was the establishment of a wage-price spiral and, eventually, rising unemployment. This toxic mix has come to be called "stagflation." The damaging social and political consequences of stagflation led President Nixon to implement the first peacetime wage and price controls in 1971, and inspired President Ford's Whip Inflation Now (WIN) campaign—both of which failed miserably and inadvertently added to the inflation psychology that gripped the country.

In 1965, inflation was just 1.6% and the jobless rate was 4.5%. Ten years later, in 1975, inflation would be 9.1% and the jobless rate would be up to 8.4%. By the summer of 1980, inflation was over 13.3% and the unemployment rate was 7.7%.

The stress stagflation imposed on households boiled over into the presidential campaign in 1980; in the end, it set the stage for the problems we confront today. In fact, the Reagan campaign turned the tables on the Carter reelection team and used Arthur Okun's "Misery index" to underscore how bad things had become for households as a result of rapidly rising inflation and joblessness.

The Misery index is calculated by simply adding the inflation rate to the unemployment rate, and the Reagan team stressed how this index had deteriorated and increased the "misery" during President Carter's tenure. This index rose to its peak of 21.98% in June 1980, up from 12.72% when President Carter took office. The growing list of economic and social problems confronting households is considered one of the key reasons why President Carter lost his reelection bid and became a rare one-term president, which ushered in the Reagan revolution and the Volcker war on inflation.

President	Time Period	Average	Low	High	Start	End	Change
Harry Truman	1945–1952	7.88	3.45–Dec 1952	13.62–Jan 1948	13.63	3.45	-10.18
Dwight D. Eisenhower	1953–1960	9.26	2.97–Jul 1953	10.96–Apr 1958	3.28	9.96	+4.68
John F. Kennedy	1961–1962	7.14	6.40–Jul 1962	8.38–Jul 1961	8.31	6.82	-1.49
Lyndon B. Johnson	1963–1968	6.77	5.70–Nov 1965	8.19–Jul 1968	7.02	8.12	+1.10
Richard Nixon	1969–1974	10.57	7.80–Jan 1969	17.01–Jul 1974	7.80	17.01	+9.21
Gerald Ford	1974–1976	16.00	12.66–Dec 1976	19.90–Jan 1975	16.36	12.66	-3.70
Jimmy Carter	1977–1980	16.26	12.60–Apr 1978	21.98–Jun 1980	12.72	19.72	+7.00
Ronald Reagan	1981–1988	12.79	7.70–Dec 1986	19.33–Jan 1981	19.33	9.72	-9.61
George H. W. Bush	1989–1992	10.68	9.64–Sep 1989	14.47–Nov 1990	10.07	10.30	+0.23
Bill Clinton	1993–2000	7.80	5.74–Apr 1998	10.56–Jan 1993	10.56	7.29	-3.27
George W. Bush	2001–2008	8.11	5.71–Oct 2006	11.47 Aug 2008	7.93	7.39	-0.54
Barack Obama	2009–Aug 2015 Incomplete Data	9.41	5.30–Aug 2015	12.97–Sep 2011	7.83	5.30	-2.53

fig 4.3

Source: Bano Misery Index, 1999

INFLATION BY THE NUMBERS

Originally reported data show that inflation averaged 6.8% in the 1970s—there were two periods during the decade where prices accelerated by double digits. These two episodes of rapidly accelerating prices, 1973–1975 and 1978–1980, were both dominated by food and energy price shocks; however, there was also a new persistence to inflation that made it a major social problem of the decade. Bad weather in the US and, more important, the rest of the world pushed the CPI for food up by 15% between 1972 and 1973 and by an additional 12% in 1974. The 1973 oil embargo quadrupled the price of crude oil imports; and, as a result of the widespread use of cost-of-living clauses in union contracts, these temporary inflation shocks were channeled directly into cost structures. As such, headline CPI accelerated by upward of 10% between 1972 and 1974, while the core or underlying inflation rate increased by more than 8% over this same period. Even though headline and core inflation slowed in 1975, these two inflation measures never returned to 1972 levels. It has been suggested that the poorly designed and executed Nixon wage and price controls contributed to this situation, but the link between wages and prices is a more compelling argument.

Food and energy prices again contributed to the 8% acceleration in inflation between 1977 and the first half of 1980, but this time rising mortgage interest rates also proved to be a big contributor to the headline and core CPI. Because the CPI is an index of current transaction prices, the Bureau of Labor Statistics (BLS) used the current market rate on new mortgages in its calculations of housing costs at that time (today the BLS uses a homeowners' equivalent rent concept, but questions about this new approach still exist). However, the rising inflation and interest rate environment triggered by a weather-related rise in beef prices and the Iranian Revolution's impact on crude oil added almost 3% to inflation during the first six months of 1980, as originally reported.

	All Items		Excluding Food and Energy	
	CPI [1]	PCE [2]	CPI [1]	PCE [2]
1972	3.4%	3.7%	3.0%	3.3%
1973	8.8%	7.3%	4.7%	4.4%
1974	12.2%	11.0%	11.3%	9.6%
1975	7.0%	6.0%	6.7%	5.7%
1976	4.8%	5.0%	6.1%	6.0%
1977	6.8%	5.9%	6.4%	6.1%
1978	9.0%	7.8%	8.5%	6.8%
1979	13.3%	9.5%	11.3%	7.1%
1980:				
First Half	14.8%	11.0%	14.6%	9.7%
Second Half	9.9%	9.1%	9.6%	8.5%

Notes: 1 Twelve months ending in December of given year
2 Four quarters ending in Fourth quarter of given year

fig 4.4

Source: Alan Blinder, Anatomy of Double Digit Inflation in the 1970s

Consequences of Inflation

Economists generally identify seven negative consequences of inflation, and these are used to justify establishing explicit inflation targets for central banks. These costs can be broken down into those that directly affect the consumer and those that indirectly affect households by distorting company behavior. Specifically, accelerating inflation increases the risks that companies face as a result of rising wage demands. The increase in unit labor costs leads to lower corporate profits and less incentive for companies to hire new workers. Business competitiveness is also reduced by rising inflation.

Inflation tends to lead to rising prices for goods and services, making them less competitive, especially in an international marketplace. Eventually this leads to reduced exports, increased imports, lower profits, and reduced job opportunities. A declining exchange rate brought about by rising prices tends to push up the cost of raw materials, further squeezing corporate profits. Business uncertainty also increases and corporate confidence declines, as companies cannot be sure of the cost structures they face.

A rising cost of borrowing is a direct negative for all economic agents. The providers of loanable funds protect their purchasing power during periods of accelerating inflation by raising the interest rates that they charge for the use of their savings. This increases the cost of financing new investments and/or the daily operations, which affects companies as well as households. Savers suffer during periods of inflation, especially if they loaned money long-term based on a lower inflation forecast.

Accelerating inflation can also squeeze real incomes. Prices are free to rise over time, but most workers are generally entitled to only one salary increase a year. In addition, inflation tends to result in a redistribution of income to borrowers from savers. Inflation imposes an indirect tax on lower-income households. These families tend to spend a disproportionate share of their income on highly volatile food- and energy-related purchases.

Besides these often-cited consequences of inflation, the establishment of a wage-price spiral in the 1970s upped the ante as cost-of-living adjustments established a feedback loop through the commodity markets that embedded an inflation psychology into the economy and resulted in the politically unacceptable environment of stagflation.

Deflationary Forces Start to Build

The pain inflicted on the economy from the combination of a wage-price spiral and rising unemployment, i.e., stagflation, triggered a series of policy initiatives designed to reverse these adverse trends. These policy changes sparked a fundamental transition in the economy that eventually shifted us from a world of excess demand to today's excess supply situation. The deflationary forces evident in the global economy are a direct result of these policies.

The embattled President Carter appointed Paul Volcker as Chairman of the Federal Reserve Board of Governors in August 1979 and made the first critical decision that started the deflationary ball rolling. The appointment of the then–New York Fed President to Chairman of the Board of Governors heralded a monetary policy shift that would have profound long-term implications for the domestic and global economy. The new Fed chairman focused principally on achieving price stability in order to promote maximum employment, even if the resulting interest rate environment clashed with the intent of fiscal policy initiatives. Technically, Chairman Volcker shifted the thrust of policy from the demand-side management advocated by Keynes to the more monetarist theories championed by Milton Friedman. The basic tenet of the monetarist philosophy is that inflation is the result of excess money supply created by the central bank. As such, the shift to money supply from interest rate targeting undertaken by Chairman Volcker reflected a clean break with the fundamental principles of monetary policy that had guided the economy in the postwar period. The result of this transition would be a dramatic rise in short-term interest rates, a steep inversion of the yield curve, and a sharp reversal in the exchange value of the dollar from depreciation to appreciation. These developments were designed to break the back of the inflation psychology that had become embedded in the economic decision-making process.

The unforeseen consequences of the Volcker war on inflation were a rapid rise in real rates that ushered in a period
of intense financial innovation and the institutionalizing of
wealth. An increased concentration of loanable funds in the
hands of professional money managers, who compete for savings balances on the basis of achieving above-market returns
for their investors, led to the belief that the double-digit returns
of the 1970s and 1980s were the norm and not the exception.
The need to deliver above-market returns supported the development of the junk bond market and the explosion in trading
mortgage-backed securities. The availability of relatively low-
cost computer analytics allowed for the explosion in the derivatives market. The struggle for double-digit returns, even after
a more stable inflation rate was reestablished, would lead to
the technology bubble in the late 1990s and early 2000s, and
subsequently, the housing bubble in the 2002–2007 period.
Unrealistic return expectations are at the heart of the excess
supply situation we confront today.

The second major development to come out of the drive
to end stagflation was the Reagan supply-side revolution. The
across-the-board tax cuts implemented during President Reagan's first term were intended to boost domestic spending and
investment in order to expand the economy (via increased
supply), and to drive increased employment. The theoretical
justification for his tax cut policies came from the empirical
work of Arthur Laffer, who suggested that beyond some opti-
mal level increasing tax rates will lead to reduced tax revenue
and a weaker economy—the Laffer curve. Conversely, cutting

tax rates would lead to more tax revenue and an expanded economy.

President Reagan's supply-side approach was multifaceted. Besides tax cuts, the Reagan administration promoted industry deregulation (transportation and telecommunication), advanced free trade, and supported labor market reforms that weakened the power of unions (air traffic controllers' strike). The guiding theme under Reagan initiatives was the principle that expanding the economy would lift the living standard of all workers. This concept came to be known as trickle-down economics.

He promoted free trade agreements, arguing that increasing the competitiveness of domestic companies would result in an increased share of overseas markets and a further increase in both domestic output and employment while helping to hold down the cost of goods and services domestically. Unfortunately, government spending cuts that were also part of the Reagan program were never implemented by Congress, and the resulting budget deficits supported the rising interest rate environment associated with Chairman Volcker's war on inflation. High real long-term rates dampened domestic investment while lower tax rates increased consumer spending and propelled the economy forward at a healthy pace. This mix of fiscal stimulus and monetary policy tightening pushed the dollar dramatically higher and resulted in an expansion in international trade—but at the expense of domestic manufacturers. The need to deliver double-digit returns, even as inflation rates declined, resulted in the

cost-cutting-to-profitability model that still dominates corporate decision making.

Companies searching for lower costs expanded in the
overseas markets, and the rising exchange value of the dollar triggered the globalization of wealth. Double-digit return
expectations led to an expansion in overseas manufacturing at
the expense of higher-cost domestic producers, and the result
was an explosion in the growth of emerging economies centered on an "export-to-growth" model.

This search for lower costs to boost profits and investor
returns stretched through Southeast Asia and Latin America
before reaching its peak with market-based reforms undertaken in China. The growth of the hedge fund community,
and the pressure on management imposed by activist shareholders, further facilitated this drive for above-market returns.

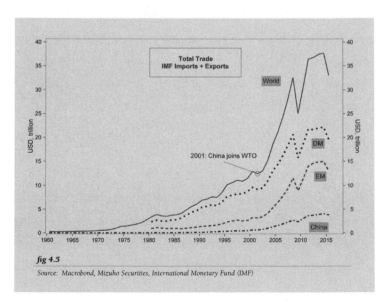

fig 4.5

Source: Macrobond, Mizuho Securities, International Monetary Fund (IMF)

The transition to excess supply from excess demand started to become evident in the early 1990s and was completed in 2007 when China opted not to fall victim to the bursting of the housing bubble, an event that plunged most of the world into a deep recession.

To avoid being affected by the global recession, China doubled down on investment spending in many of the industries where it was already invested heavily. The result was an increase in the excess capacity of industries that provide tradable goods, especially those targeted at the consumer. The raw material producers also overbuilt during this period, as confidence in China's ability to continue to grow at double-digit rates was never questioned. The growth of China into arguably the largest or second-largest economy should have been seen as evidence that sustained double-digit growth was no longer possible. However, the drive to attain above-market returns was so strong that raw material producers overbuilt capacity as well in an effort to show sustained growth. The post-2007 stimulus in China was also funded by debt that left the economy with a lot of bad loans to deal with, further dampening its growth potential. The regulatory reforms undertaken by the developed economies in the wake of the 2007 financial crises—especially in Europe and the US—further exacerbated the excess supply situation by limiting the ability of households to borrow; meanwhile, companies saw no reason to invest in new plants or equipment due to excess supply.

This resulted in a global economy lacking both a driver and/or momentum. The net effect of these trends is the debt/

deflation spiral, which has and will continue to dominate central bank decisions until aggressive demand-side strategies are eventually adopted to correct the fundamental imbalance. Although the Fed is currently not confronting deflation domestically, the risk is forcing policy to be supportive well into the ongoing expansion. This shift in policy recognizes that inflation no longer drives the business cycle—credit does—and in this environment, the Fed no longer needs to take the punch bowl away before the party gets started. Instead, the FOMC has to leave the punch bowl on the table until the party gets a good buzz going.

Volcker Shifts to Monetary Aggregate Targeting

The dramatic rise in inflation between 1965 and 1980 elicited a shift in fundamental precepts of macroeconomic theory and the assumptions of how policy should be implemented to achieve maximum employment. The concept of an exploitable trade-off between inflation and unemployment as envisioned by the Keynesian approach was replaced by the monetarist doctrine that assumed the key to healthy long-term growth was not a monetary policy validation of fiscal policy initiatives, but rather stable growth in the monetary aggregates. Inflation was seen as the result of excessive money supply growth. Although there is still considerable debate over whether the policies implemented by the Federal Reserve under Chairman Volcker were truly a shift to orthodox monetarist principles, there is no doubt that the Fed's monetary policy decisions undertaken during his tenure had a profound effect on the economy, inflation, inflation expectations, financial markets, and most importantly, return expectations—all of which helped transition the economy from a world of excess demand to one of excess supply.

Paul Volcker was appointed chairman of the Federal Reserve Board by President Carter in August 1979 following a cabinet shakeup at the White House that moved then–Chairman Miller to the head of the Treasury Department. At the time of his appointment, the new chairman had been president of the New York Federal Reserve Bank. Prior to being at the New York Fed, Paul Volcker served as undersecretary of the Treasury for international monetary affairs under President Nixon. In this capacity, he had been instrumental in the August 1971 decision to suspend gold convertibility, which resulted in the collapse of the Bretton Woods System. After leaving the Treasury he became president of the New York Fed in 1975, which gave him valuable insight into the thought process of the FOMC and its decisions as inflation ratcheted upwards in the second half of the decade.

During his confirmation hearings, the future chairman pledged to make fighting inflation his top priority. At the time, inflation was running around 9%; gold and silver prices were rising rapidly (22.7% and 8.5%, respectively, over the first six months of the year); and the dollar was also under significant downward pressure. During the first six months of 1979, the broad dollar index declined by 8.7% as the FOMC continued to allow inflation pressures to build in light of evidence that the economy was stagnating. This situation reached a breaking point in the fall of that year. Chairman Volcker returned from an IMF meeting in Belgrade in early October and decided that action had to be taken to bring inflation under control. At the IMF meeting, his European counterparts expressed deep concern about the destabilizing effects of the declining dollar and the accelerating inflation spiral that was evident in the data. In fact, the recently released August CPI data showed a 12% annualized increase in the core price measure, up from 8.7% the month before. This situation set the stage for a decisive break in direction for monetary policy.

At a special, unannounced FOMC meeting held on Saturday, October 6, 1979, the Committee shifted from interest rate to money supply targeting. This abrupt shift in the Fed's intermediate policy target allowed for greater volatility in the Fed funds rate as the Committee focused its actions on gaining control over inflation, which was seen as a direct consequence of excessive money supply growth. The need for better control of money growth was clear in the third quarter of that year. Over the July to September period, M1[1] had grown at more than a 9% annualized rate—this is in comparison to the Fed's target of just 1.5% to 4.5% for this narrow money supply measure. M2 had grown at an annual rate of 12% during the same

---

1   See text box beginning on page 106 for explanation of M1, M2, etc.

three-month period. The Committee had been expecting this broader measure to grow by a more moderate 5% to 8%.

Accordingly, the Committee, which previously could not agree to hike rates, decided that "the situation called for additional measures to restrain growth of the monetary aggregates." The result was a substantial widening in the acceptable range for the fed funds rate. At the FOMC meeting in September, a 50 basis point range was set for the fed funds rate of 11.25% to 11.75%. Just one month later, at the October meeting, this range was increased to 400 basis points, from 11.5% to 15.5%. The wider band was established to provide the New York Open Market Desk flexibility to establish a path for bank reserves that was consistent with achieving the Committee's desired rates of growth for the monetary aggregates. Essentially, the level of short-term rates was now allowed to seek whatever level was necessary to bring the demand for reserves in line with the path for non-borrowed reserves that was consistent with the Committee's money supply objective. The target zone for the monetary aggregates would be adjusted downward over time in order to gradually return inflation to a more sustainable path.

In response to these changes, the fed funds rate rose sharply, and by year-end it was almost 15%. The funds rate peaked out at almost 20% in March of 1980. More important, the spike in short rates inverted the yield curve, or the spread between the funds rate and the 10-year Treasury note, by more than 700 basis points at its widest. This inversion would lead to a deep recession; and in the process, it would alter investors' return expectations and behavior.

MONEY AND THE MONETARY AGGREGATES

The quantity theory of money was used to justify the shift from interest rates to money supply targeting orchestrated by Chairman Volcker. The monetarist approach to setting policy is based on a simple identity: $M\%+V\%=P\%+Q\%$. This identity suggests that nominal output growth, $P\%+Q\%$, or price growth plus output growth, is equal to $M\%+V\%$, or money growth plus the rate of turnover in money. If you assume that in the short run the rate of turnover of money and real output are both constant, then the inflation rate is determined by the rate of growth of the money. However, in order to implement this approach, the FOMC needed to define money. The quantity theory assumes that money is simply the medium of exchange, but, in practice, it is also a store of value.

As far back as 1944, the Federal Reserve Board began reporting monthly data on currency in the hands of the nonbank public and the level of non-interest-bearing demand deposits held at banks. Demand deposits were seen as being easily convertible into cash. Up until 1971, M1, or the sum of these two measures of transaction balances, was the only monetary aggregate calculated by the Fed. That year the Fed also began publishing data on M2 and M3, incorporating a temporary store of value concept into the monetary aggregates. M2 was defined as M1 plus savings deposits and time deposits at commercial banks, excluding large negotiable CDs. M3 added deposits at mutual savings banks and those at savings and loan associations to M2. By 1975, even broader measures of money were being calculated—M4 and M5.

Financial innovation was also blurring the lines between the Ms in the 1970s. Banks began offering new deposit accounts that were close substitutes for demand deposits, but which paid interest—NOW, or negotiable order of withdrawal accounts. Savings accounts with automatic transfers to checking—ATS accounts—were also introduced. Credit union share drafts and money market mutual funds with check-writing privileges were also being introduced. These new accounts were being used as transactions accounts, but were not counted in M1. These deficiencies were addressed in 1980 when the Federal Reserve Board redefined the aggregates. M1 was replaced by M1A and M1B. M1A was the old M1, but M1B now included NOW and ATS balances at banks and thrift institutions as well as credit union share drafts and demand deposits at mutual savings banks. M2 now included M1B and a number of asset types that were easily convertible into cash. These included overnight repurchase agreements issued by commercial banks, overnight Eurodollars held by nonbank US residents, money market fund shares, and savings and small time deposits at all depository institutions. M1B was the primary money supply target of the Volcker Fed, even though ranges were also published for the broader aggregates compiled by the board.

FEDS NON-BORROWED RESERVES OPERATING PROCEDURES

The shift orchestrated by Chairman Volcker in October 1979 required not only a change in the intermediate policy target, but also a fundamental change in the workings of the reserve market. Under the prior model, the FOMC pegged the level of the fed funds rate at a number they thought would achieve both stable prices and maximum employment.

In practice, however, the politicized nature of changes in the funds rate meant interest rate changes were more reactive than anticipatory. As a result, the FOMC tended to accommodate increases in the demand for reserves in order to avoid an unintended increase in the funds rate. This dynamic assured that a rightward shift in the demand for reserves, associated with an increase in money supply, was immediately accommodated by the manager of the Open Market Desk of the New York Fed through an increase in the supply of non-borrowed reserves. Essentially, the supply of reserves to the banking system became perfectly elastic at the target fed funds rate, and any deviation in the money supply beyond the Committee's desired rate was accommodated.

The shift to money supply targeting led to a decidedly less elastic supply of reserves. To avoid accommodating every increase in the demand for reserves, the Committee had to establish a path for non-borrowed reserves that would be consistent with a gradual slowing in money growth. Any increase in the demand for reserves that exceeded the level of non-borrowed reserves consistent with the Committee's money supply target would now necessitate a rise in the fed funds

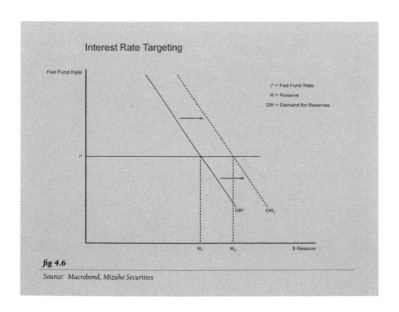

fig 4.6

Source: Macrobond, Mizuho Securities

rate, as banks are forced into the discount window—which there is a natural reluctance to use.

As such, there tends to be a positive relationship between the volume of reserves that banks will borrow from the discount window and the spread between the fed funds rate and the discount rate. The greater the volume of borrowed reserves required due to an unanticipated increase in money supply, the wider the spread—or the higher the fed funds rate. This means that the fed funds rate automatically reacts to an unanticipated increase in the money supply, creating a feedback loop through the transactions demand for money that slows the economy and returns money supply growth toward its target.

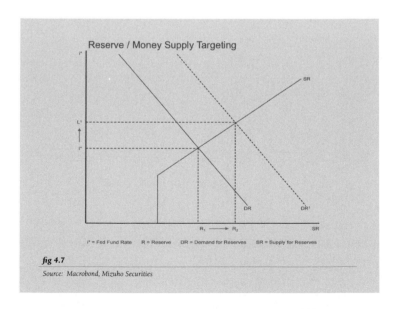

Reserve / Money Supply Targeting

i* = Fed Fund Rate   R = Reserve   DR = Demand for Reserves   SR = Supply for Reserves

fig 4.7

Source: Macrobond, Mizuho Securities

Recession of 1980

The sharp increase in short-term interest rates and the inversion of the yield curve that followed the Volcker policy shift led to deep back-to-back recessions in 1980 and again in 1981. The temporary implementation of credit controls by the Carter administration is largely credited with the six-month 1980 recession, while the longer 1981–1982 contraction is generally seen as being caused by the Volcker war on inflation. The Fed did contribute, however, to the 1980 contraction by instituting a new, special reserve requirement on bank deposits in an attempt to reduce excess reserves in the banking system and by adding a surcharge on a portion of bank discount window borrowings. These steps had an unexpectedly large, combined negative effect on the economy and had to be reversed quickly to counteract the damage being done. The 1980 recession pulled real GDP down by 2.2%—from peak to trough—over just six months. Industrial production collapsed by 6.6% and the S&P 500 fell by 17.1%. The easing of the Carter credit controls and a reversal of the Fed tightening later that year allowed the economy to snap back, and rates moved sharply higher again. Real GDP bounced 4.4% and the S&P rallied by more than 40%.

The speed and breadth of the bounce surprised policy makers, and the result was a second sharp reversal in the direction of monetary policy. This time the policy tightening lasted until the end of 1982, driving up the jobless rate to almost 11% and the fed funds rate to more than 19% before it ended. The recession lasted 16 months, the longest postwar downturn to date; and real GDP fell by 2.5% as stocks tumbled almost 30% peak to trough. The back-to-back recession volatility experienced in financial markets resulted in two important developments: First, the high yields offered by money market instruments and the explosive flow into money market mutual funds triggered the institutionalization of wealth; and second, the Reagan political revolution began, which focused on increasing the supply of goods and services as a cure for inflation over the Fed's demand-side management.

The inherent conflict between Reagan's fiscal and Volcker's monetary policy led to a dramatic rise in real rates across the entire maturity spectrum. This and the equity market rally that followed the 1980 and 1981 recessions altered the fundamentals of retirement investing and return expectations, which have led to today's excess supply situation.

Institutionalization and Globalization of Wealth

The 1980s proved to be an important transition decade for the US economy. Not only did inflation spiral out of control as the economy stagnated, but the resulting monetary and fiscal policy response led to a fundamental shift in the ways in which the government, companies, and households approach saving and investing for retirement. The Volcker war on inflation and the Reagan supply-side approach to fiscal policy altered the fundamental paths of both the domestic and global economies, and brought about the shift from a world of excess demand to that of excess supply.

This shift was becoming apparent as far back as 1990, but it has only recently gained recognition by a handful of policy makers. A key aspect of this transition was the increased concentration of wealth being managed by professional money managers. These money managers competed for household and corporate savings balances based on their promise to deliver above-market returns to investors. This ignited a trend toward shareholder activism, which forced companies to manage for the current benefit of shareholders rather than anticipated future gains. The confluence of these powerful trends spawned the institutionalization and the globalization of wealth. Although the efficiencies brought about by institutionalization and globalization were a decided positive for the economy at the time, the unintended consequences proved the old adage "too much of a good thing is no good for you."

The institutionalization of wealth can be traced to the damaging effect that stagflation had on retirement savings. Accelerating inflation reduced the purchasing power of retirees living on fixed incomes, while equity market performance suffered in the wake of the oil embargo early in the decade, and the spike in interest rates later in the decade. The back-to-back recessions of the early 1980s were also key developments in the process of institutionalizing wealth by professional money managers.

The financial stress of creeping inflation on retirees was already evident in the late 1960s, and it resulted in a series of Social Security benefit increases very early in the decade and the introduction of an automatic cost-of-living adjustment, or COLA, in 1972. The combination of the expanding role of Social Security, the introduction of a minimum benefit, and the Supplemental Security Income program quickly brought the solvency of the program into question. These and other changes made Social Security the primary retirement plan for many households.

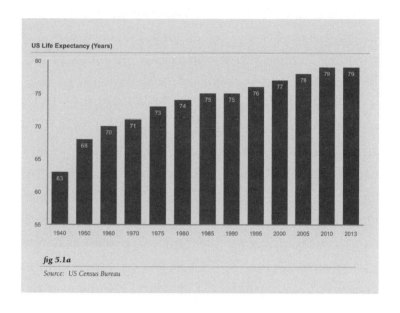

fig 5.1a

Source: *US Census Bureau*

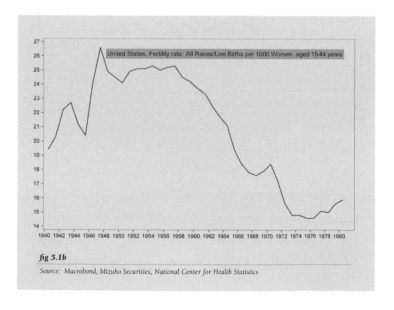

fig 5.1b

Source: *Macrobond, Mizuho Securities, National Center for Health Statistics*

Unfortunately, the government-sponsored program quickly ran into the demographic realities of a slowing birthrate and stagnating incomes. The clear financial weakness in the program's structure had a powerful effect on household psychology and turned the solvency of the retirement scheme into a major political issue. The need to generate increased retirement savings to supplement Social Security prompted the introduction of Individual Retirement Accounts (IRAs) in 1974. The use of IRAs expanded dramatically in the 1980s when the Economic Recovery Tax Act of 1981 allowed all working taxpayers, regardless of their coverage under another qualified retirement plan, to contribute to an IRA. The 401(k) corporate retirement plan, which is now the primary retirement plan for most private workers, was also part of the same legislation.

SOCIAL SECURITY SYSTEM BAILOUT

The Great Depression was the catalyst for the Social Security Act of 1935, which was signed into law by President Roosevelt. The Act created several programs that today form the basis for the government's income-security safety net. These include the old-age insurance fund, unemployment insurance, and aid to families with dependent children. The original legislation also provided federal funding for means-tested old-age assistance provided by states, which would eventually become the Supplemental Security Income program.

Initially, the all-important retirement benefit was payable only to persons aged 65 and older who were no longer working. Program benefits were constrained by a retirement earnings test that limited those who could collect a monthly benefit to retirees earning less than $15 a month. The movement toward universal coverage was slow and evolved through a series of reforms undertaken during the program's first fifteen years.

By 1950, estimates indicate that a full 60% of the population was covered by the Social Security program, making it the primary retirement system— rather than simply providing a safety net for the poorest households. Nine years later, 86% of the population was covered by Social Security. The monthly benefit formula remained unchanged until 1950 when Congress enacted a 77% increase in the monthly payment to bring the system in line with retiree needs. Three additional increases were enacted between 1951 and 1959, totaling 32.5%. The Disability Insurance program was also added in 1959, but only for workers aged 50 through 64. Today disability is available to workers of all ages.

Over the next ten years, Social Security benefit payments continued to increase, with the basic retirement payment rising by 20% through two separate changes in the formula. Significant increases were also passed for widows and survivors; however, the big increase in the scope of the government's safety net was the addition of the Medicare program in 1965. Benefit expansion continued in the early 1970s, with the addition of a special minimum benefit payment and a 25% increase in the monthly benefit in each of the first two years of the new decade. A final 20% increase was enacted in 1972, and a new automatic cost-of-living adjustment was legislated. The result of all these changes was that Social Security rapidly became a central aspect of all retirement planning; so when questions concerning the solvency of the system surfaced later in the decade, they reverberated throughout the economy and helped trigger a change in behavior that precipitated the shift from excess demand to excess supply.

The solvency issue was such a deep social and political concern that President Reagan appointed a special commission chaired by Alan Greenspan to recommend changes in the program to ensure its solvency. The stagflation environment of the 1970s not only negatively affected the private retirement plans, but the lack of wage increases and the overly generous automatic cost-of-living adjustments in benefits helped increase the program from 3% in 1970 to 5% of GDP in 1982. The Greenspan commission made a series of recommendations that were adopted by Congress in the 1983 amendments to the system. These included expanding the program's tax base by including newly hired federal workers, subjecting a portion of Social Security benefits to income taxation, accelerating scheduled increases in the payroll tax, and delaying cost-of-living adjustments by six months from June to December each year.

Despite these changes, and the fact that the system would now be in surplus for many years to come, the detailed analysis of the system's flawed model made it clear that the retirement of the "baby boomers" would create a politically unacceptable strain on "generation X" and "millennials." This actuarial deficiency strongly implied that the program's benefits would have to be curtailed at some point in the not-so-distant future, leading many workers to believe that they would

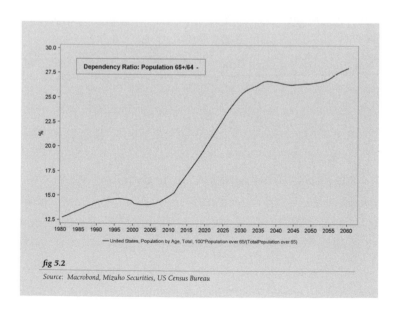

fig 5.2

Source: *Macrobond, Mizuho Securities, US Census Bureau*

never get out of the system anywhere near what they had paid in.

The problem simply is that Social Security is really an intergenerational transfer payment. Money invested by the program in non-marketable government securities is spent by the government on current expenditures and will have to be redeemed with future tax revenue.

Internationalization of Wealth

The concentration of savings balances in the hands of professional money managers was initially triggered by Regulation Q restrictions on the banking system's ability to pay interest on savings and transactions accounts. Regulation Q not only prohibited banks from paying interest on transactions accounts, but it also limited the interest payments on savings accounts. The original purpose behind Regulation Q was a belief that bank failures of the 1930s were due, in part, to excessive bank competition for funds. By the 1960s, however, the purpose of Regulation Q had transitioned to an attempt to stimulate bank mortgage lending by holding down the cost of bank funding. The general rise in rates during the 1960s and 1970s, however, had more to do with the demand for funds generated by the excess demand for goods and services than from banks competing for funds.

The caps imposed by Regulation Q instead encouraged the development of alterative savings vehicles, including Money Market Mutual Funds (MMFs). This highly liquid investment alternative emerged in 1971, and by 1982 accounted for 76% of all mutual fund assets. In fact, the growth of the mutual fund industry can be directly traced to the Volcker war on inflation, the expansion of IRAs, the development of 401(k)s, and the 1976 law that allowed mutual funds to pass through tax-exempt income to investors, and, in effect, spawned the municipal money fund industry.

The phenomenal growth of the mutual fund industry was first evident in the money markets. The number of money market

Year	Number of Money Market Mutual Funds		MMMY Assets Billions	
	Taxable	Tax-exempt	Taxable	Tax Exempt
1974	15			
1975	36		3.7	
1976	48		3.69	
1977	50		3.89	
1978	61		10.86	
1979	78		45.53	
1980	106		76.36	
1981	179		186.16	
1982	310		219.84	
1983	373		179.39	
1984	331	94	209.75	23.8
1985	350	110	207.55	36.25
1986	360	127	228.35	63.81
1987	389	154	254.68	61.42
1988	433	177	272.2	65.76
1989	470	203	358.62	69.47
1990	505	236	414.56	83.78
1991	552	268	452.46	89.98
1992	585	279	451.35	94.84
1993	627	293	461.88	103.44
1994	649	314	501.11	109.98
1995	676	321	631.32	121.69
1996	669	319	763.94	137.87
1997	685	328	901.23	157.66
1998	687	339	1166.97	184.71
1999	704	341	1413.25	199.9
2000	704	335	1611.38	233.87
2001	690	325	2026.23	259.08
2002	677	311	1988.78	276.3
2003	660	313	1749.73	290.29
2004	639	305	1589.7	312
2005	593	277	1690.45	336.37
2006	573	274	1969.42	369.03
2007	545	260	2617.67	468.09
2008	534	249	3338.56	493.58
2009	476	228	2916.96	398.94
2010	442	210	2473.51	330.01
2011	431	201	2399.25	291.7
2012	400	180	2405.74	287.43
2013	382	173	2447.2	270.61
2014	364	163	2463.85	260.79
2015	336	145	2499.81	254.93

fig 5.3

Source: *Investment Company Institute*

funds expanded from just 15 in 1974 to 318 in 1982, or 71% of the increase in all mutual funds over this ten-year period. The assets held by money market funds also expanded dramatically. Mutual fund assets expanded by $215 billion between 1975 and 1982 while the assets under management of the total industry increased by $251 billion. When savers and investors realized that higher returns could be achieved, there was no going back; and the institutionalization of wealth was now a fundamental trend in the economy—with powerful consequences.

As the economy slipped into the deep and long 1981–1982 recession, the Fed was forced to ease. Short-term rates declined and return-addicted investors responded. The result was a

	Number of Equity Mutual Funds Number		Assets Billions	
	Domestic	Global	Domestic	Global
1974				
1975	343		37.49	
1976	314		39.19	
1977	302		34.07	
1978	296		32.67	
1979	294		35.88	
1980	289		44.42	
1981	288		41.19	
1982	306		53.63	
1983	340		76.97	
1984	396	29	74.55	23.8
1985	430	43	103.39	36.25
1986	519	57	138.98	63.81
1987	621	81	158.02	61.42
1988	743	109	171.4	65.76
1989	897	128	221.45	69.47
1990	941	155	211.18	83.78
1991	944	206	365.21	89.98
1992	985	239	468.41	94.84
1993	1086	306	626.54	103.44
1994	1280	423	691.57	109.89
1995	1463	528	1052.57	121.69
1996	1611	668	1440.81	137.87
1997	1902	768	2021.66	157.66
1998	2183	890	2586.31	184.71
1999	2622	949	3456.64	199.9
2000	3004	1055	3369.73	233.87
2001	3315	1085	2947.93	259.08
2002	3610	1018	2273.05	376.3
2003	3714	929	3118.32	290.29
2004	3659	887	3626.37	312
2005	3651	912	3929.72	336.37
2006	3659	995	4472.13	369.03
2007	3748	1060	4694.65	468.09
2008	3678	1140	2738.82	493.68
2009	3655	1172	3564.56	398.94
2010	3419	1194	4053.93	330.01
2011	3321	1266	3855.4	291.7
2012	3259	1279	4324.64	287.43
2013	3217	1345	5726.85	270.61
2014	3238	1410	6233.17	260.79
2015	3277	1487	6045.88	254.93

fig 5.4

Source: *Investment Company Institute*

contraction in money market fund assets as investors sought out alternative savings strategies. In 1983, the number of money market mutual funds offered increased by 55 to 373, but the assets under management by MMFs dipped by over $40 billion. Declining market rates, the Reagan tax cuts, the expansion in defense spending, the move toward deregulation, the decline in labor union influence, a push for free trade, a resurgence in confidence, and the drive to make publicly traded companies accountable to shareholders all resulted in a powerful equity market rally. The broad market index, in fact, rose from an August 1982 low of just 102.41 to just under 170 at the end of 1984, for a 63.3% increase. The rally experienced in the narrow Dow Jones Industrials was equally impressive. The yield on the 10-year Treasury benchmark peaked in late September 1981 at 16%, but ended 1982 just below the 10.5% level. This decline in bond yields and the rise in the price of fixed-income securities also caused an increase in savings balances flowing into bond mutual funds.

The rally in both stocks and bonds attracted mutual fund managers who were quick to react, and they began to aggressively market their equity and bond fund alternatives. These higher-fee products remain the backbone of the mutual fund industry today. Of the 8,116 mutual funds in existence in 2015, more than half were equity funds, while about one in four were bond funds. The industry has grown to $15.7 trillion in 2015 from $371 billion in 1984. The story sold to investors was simple and direct: Professional fund managers would search out domestic companies that could deliver above-market returns and use their research abilities, market knowledge, influence over management, and buying power to find the next hot growth companies, and/or unlock value in companies, and thus generate double-digit returns for investors.

The average stock fund return over the 1983–2003 period was a very healthy 10.3%. Since the burst of the technology bubble in 2001 and the crises of the financial markets in 2007, returns have been less robust for the industry in general. Although we expect that lower returns will continue, the current excess supply situation is a direct result of the search for double-digit investment returns.

The growth of shareholder activism and the migration from defined-benefit to defined-contribution pension schemes provided a significant additional push toward the institutionalization of wealth. Defined-benefit plans dominated the pension fund industry at the end of the 1970s. But as companies worked through the math of continuing to provide retirement benefits along with the emphasis on cost cutting required by managing for earnings, there was a concerted effort to end defined-benefits programs. Companies shifted employees to defined-contribution plans under the guise that workers could better provide for their own retirement by investing in a diversified portfolio of stocks and bonds, rather than relying on corporate pension plans, which tended to concentrate their investments in the parent company's obligations. A full 28% of workers participating in employment-based plans in 1979 were defined benefits. As of 2011, this share was down to just 3%. Defined-contribution plans, on the other hand, accounted for just 7% of covered workers in 1979, but have grown to more than 30% of the market. The share of workers participating in both style programs held roughly steady at around 10% through this period. The shift in the share of private sector plans was even more dramatic with defined-benefit plans dropping from 62% of the market to just 7%, while defined-contribution plans have swelled from 16% to 69%.

The shareholder activism movement accelerated dramatically in the early 1980s when corporate raiders such as Carl Icahn and T. Boone Pickens gained notoriety. Leveraged buyout firms had been around since the 1960s when Kohlberg, Kravis and Roberts began acquiring small private companies that lacked an exit strategy and had founders that did not want to sell out to competitors. Icahn and Pickens took the business a step further in their search for double-digit returns by unlocking value in poorly managed and/or vulnerable publicly traded companies. These proactive investors acquired an equity stake in publicly owned companies and forced them to take actions to increase earnings and the stock price, typically by cutting costs.

A more recent example is the dispute between Paul Singer of Elliott Management and the board of Hess Oil. Singer pushed the board of Hess for a sale of the company and/or asset sales to increase the company's stock price. Alternatively, a raider can also earn a fat premium from an embattled board of directors that opts to fight the raiders by buying back their shares at a significant premium. Carl Icahn's investment in B.F. Goodrich is a prime example. Leveraged buyout firms ballooned in the 1980s with the growth of the junk bond market cultivated by Michael Milken and Fred Joseph of Drexel Burnham Lambert.

The growth of private equity firms is another example of the search for double-digit returns. Deals such as William Simon's purchase of Gibson Greetings in late 1983 furthered the media frenzy around these high return/high risk alternative investment styles, but all of the media hype was about the return—not the risk. The $80 million investment in Gibson turned into a $290 million IPO in just sixteen months. Incredible returns attracted widespread media attention, adding to the belief that above-market returns were out there, waiting to be found. As a result, it is estimated that between 1970 and 1989, the number of leveraged buyout firms increased to more than 2000, all valued in excess of $250 million.

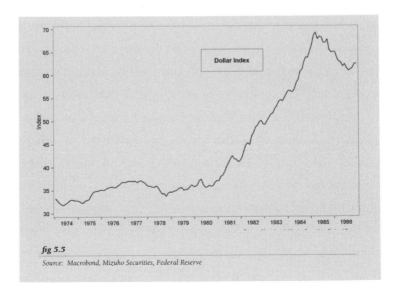

fig 5.5

Source: Macrobond, Mizuho Securities, Federal Reserve

Globalization of Wealth

The cost-cutting model employed by most leverage buyout and/or private equity firms forced this model on all domestic companies as a first line of defense against a hostile takeover. The result was a combination of higher returns across the board, reinforcing the trend toward institutionalized wealth. Eventually the ability to squeeze costs out of the domestic production process reached its limits, and companies were forced to look elsewhere for cost savings. The push into overseas economies and markets in the search for even cheaper production costs was aided by Reagan's drive for deregulation and free trade. But the sharp rise in the dollar, experienced in the wake of the inherent conflict between the liberal fiscal policy of the Reagan years and the tight monetary policy under Volcker and his predecessor, Alan Greenspan, fueled the move overseas in search of lower production costs.

The average value of the dollar relative to other major world currencies more than doubled between the end of 1979 and its peak in September 1985, when global finance ministers met at the Plaza Hotel in New York and agreed on coordinated intervention to halt the dollar's rise. The strength of the currency increased competition and the hollowing out of the US factory sector, which was becoming a political liability. The reduction in high-paying factory jobs, along with the growing influence of foreign investors in the government bond market attracted by higher real yields, marked the beginning of the globalization of wealth.

In 1985, assets of global equity mutual funds were just

under $8 billion. By 1990, that number had grown to over
$28 billion, while global bond funds had climbed to $120 billion. Later in the decade, geopolitical events set the stage for a
bigger push overseas. Specifically, the Berlin Wall fell in 1989,
and by 1990, German reunification was underway. Shortly
thereafter, in 1991, the USSR disintegrated and Boris Yeltsin
became the first president of Russia. These moves established
the US as the sole superpower, and a new optimism pushed
companies and investors beyond traditional borders.

The globalization of wealth accelerated in the 1990s as
Congress ratified the North American Free Trade Agreement
(NAFTA) in 1992, which created a trilateral trade bloc in North
America. The 1990s also saw a big push into Asia. Building on
the successes in Korea and Taiwan, the economies of Malay-
sia, Vietnam, and China all became beneficiaries of the search

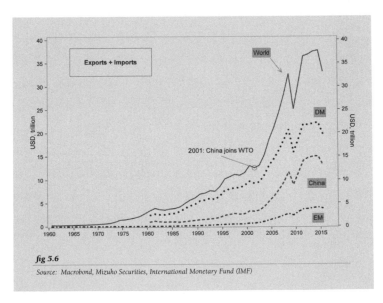

fig 5.6

Source: Macrobond, Mizuho Securities, International Monetary Fund (IMF)

for higher investment returns in growth areas as companies searched for cheaper sources of goods. The UK made the decision to return Hong Kong to China in 1997; the result was a surge in global investing and GDP. Over the ten years through 1999, global equity mutual funds ballooned to $585.3 billion while domestic equity funds surged to $3.4 trillion on strong returns. The hedge fund industry also saw impressive growth over the 1990s as the space swelled to almost 4,000 funds and assets climbed to some $500 billion.

The push to continue to cut costs in order to drive up earnings stimulated growth in overseas economies. Developing regions experienced an infusion of liquidity as manufacturers pushed into lower-cost markets to source goods and services. These countries experienced a rapid rise in real GDP, which reinforced the globalization trend as investors poured even more money into these hot new markets in the never ending search for double-digit returns. The result was an explosion in overseas investments in new plant and equipment outfitted with the latest technology to further boost the revenue that could be dropped to the almighty bottom line. In other words, the drive for sustaining the period of double-digit returns through outsourcing stimulated the transition to excess supply, and the globalization of wealth facilitated this development.

Emerging market economies experienced accelerated growth again early in the new millennium as China accelerated its push beyond its agrarian roots to avoid the fate of the USSR. China's enormous population and the central government's

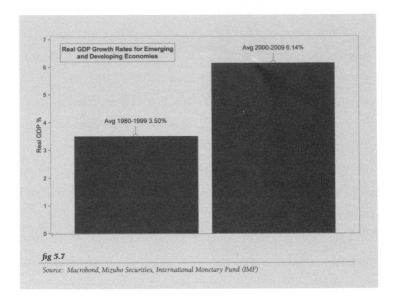

fig 5.7

Source: Macrobond, Mizuho Securities, International Monetary Fund (IMF)

willingness to adopt aspects of capitalism set the stage for the next wave of dramatic emerging market growth between 2000 and 2009, exacerbating the ability of the world economy to produce more goods and services than could be consumed under a double-digit return requirement.

These powerful trends toward institutionalization and the globalization of wealth in the search for above-market returns saw another boost from the policies introduced by President Bill Clinton, beginning in 1993 with the passage of his tax-increase program and his administration's attempt to reform the health care system. President Clinton also pushed to end welfare, which helped keep the double-digit return mentality alive by forcing more workers into the job market and cementing double-digit return expectations as a key pillar of the investment process. The 1993 IRS decision to apply carried interest rules to hedge fund managers' income led to a dramatic increase in this aggressive style for money management, furthering the double-digit return expectation model as these money managers invested aggressively in new technology companies and emerging economies. Both added to the rapid growth of supply relative to demand, which was becoming more and more constrained by the activist cost-cutting strategy and the aging of the population, not just in the developed world but also in China.

The Clinton tax hike built upon the Bush administration's decision to break its "no new taxes" pledge to secure the "pay-as-you-go" budget approach, which ended the Reagan era of an unchecked deficit-spending approach to fiscal policy. The across-the-board tax hike passed by Congress in 1993 unleashed a wave of buying of long-term bonds by hedge fund managers who saw the prospects for declining deficits as increasing the value of higher-yielding long-term bonds. The rise of the bond hedge fund managers was rapid, and the collapse of Long-Term Capital Management (LTCM) in 1998 revealed how far the search for above-market returns had pushed bond investors into even riskier strategies.

Declining long-term real rates resulted in a windfall for companies and investors as domestic and overseas opportunities became more affordable. The attempt by the Clinton administration to control health care costs in order to expand coverage provided the perfect cover for domestic companies to force workers into more cost-effective alternatives, like HMOs, under the promise of reduced out-of-pocket expenses and improved services. This dropped more revenue straight to the bottom line in the never-ending search for double-digit returns. Lower interest rates and growth of the hedge fund community led to the push into new digital technology and overseas supply chains for the next wave of cost savings.

PAY-AS-YOU-GO

Most historians will see the Gulf War as the crowning moment of the George H.W. Bush presidency, but the decision by the 41st occupant of the Oval Office to break his "no new taxes" pledge was probably the most important economic development of his term— and not just because it cost him reelection two years later. A combination of the drag on tax revenue from the 1990–1991 recession and the steady rise in non-discretionary government spending quickly pitted the Bush administration against its own party. The budget-deficit control process of across-the-board spending cuts required under the Gramm–Rudman Balanced Budget Act was politically unacceptable. Steep cuts in key social programs like Medicare and Social Security, as well as in defense, left the administration with little choice but to hike taxes.

Faced with a choice between two bad alternatives, the Bush team caved on its "no new taxes" pledge, which angered the conservative wing of the Republican Party. Initially, the president proposed only an

increase in excise taxes on gasoline; but when this pro-
posal failed in Congress, an increase in the tax rate
applied to upper-income households was added to
attract enough Democratic votes to get the bill through
Congress. The compromise was a new budget-control
process. The Bush team negotiated a new procedure
whereby all increases in direct spending or decreases
in revenue had to be offset by other spending decreases
or revenue increases. This new process would prove to
be a powerful tool, keeping government spending on
a sustainable trajectory throughout the Clinton years,
and it would help to bring real long-term rates down
after years of high real rates having hollowed out the
economy.

The dot-com craze and the power of the Internet as a
cost-effective means for delivering products across a wide
range of traditional industries was an outgrowth of the search
for double-digit returns. The cost savings embedded in this
new technology furthered the shift to excess supply from
excess demand, as did the increased use of technology in
the workplace. Desktop computers significantly reduced the
number of workers needed in administrative functions. Robotics revolutionized the factory floor in the 1980s as desktops
began to alter the way offices and retailing were structured. By
the 1990s, the Internet had broadened the use of information

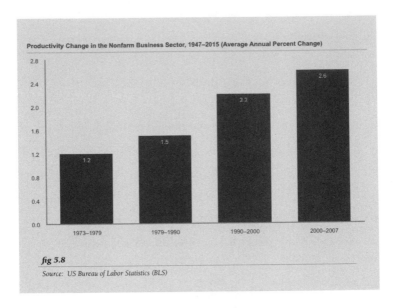

fig 5.8

Source: US Bureau of Labor Statistics (BLS)

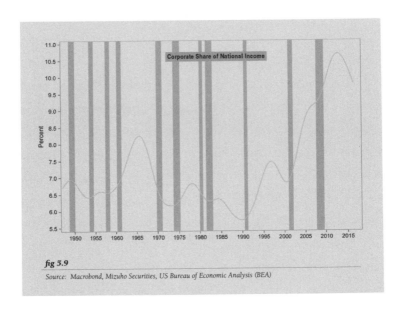

fig 5.9

Source: Macrobond, Mizuho Securities, US Bureau of Economic Analysis (BEA)

technology into many other areas, but especially in the distribution of consumer products and services.

Evidence of the effects these new technologies had on the economy and corporate earnings can be seen in the US labor productivity data. The growth of the Internet accelerated the integration of computers, which had been slowly working their way into the workplace since the 1960s, resulting in a dramatic rise in productivity. Nonfarm labor productivity accelerated to 2.2% in the 1990s from just 1.2% in the 1970s, and peaked at 2.6% from 2000–2007. The result was an acceleration in the underlying growth rate of the economy and, with it, the ability of companies to increase returns and shareholder value.

The advance in productivity should have led to a rise in living standards, as did the 2.8% spike in productivity during the 1947–1973 period; but it did not. Rather, this surge in productivity increased profitability at the expense of labor. As such, the share of national income accruing to the corporate sector rose to record highs, even as the economy tumbled during the Great Recession of 2007–2009. Allowing households to expand leverage, especially through the housing industry under the Clinton and Bush II administrations, initially masked this squeeze in labor income. Eventually the resulting housing bubble burst, and the excess supply that had been building in the global economy surfaced with a vengeance.

The growth of the hedge fund industry accelerated this transition by focusing the investment and business community on increasing shareholders' value, or, in other words, returns. As a result, the influence of the hedge fund industry expanded rapidly, as did its size. The hedge fund industry added almost 7,000 new funds between 2002 and 2007, while assets under management surged to just under $2 trillion in that year. Mutual fund assets continued to grow at a rapid rate through this period. Although the number of mutual funds held steady between 2002 and 2007, assets under management doubled to $12 trillion.

The final factor contributing to the shift from excess demand to excess supply was the decision by China not to fall into the global meltdown that gripped the world economy in late 2007. The globalization of wealth indirectly allowed the Chinese government to borrow extensively in order to provide enough stimulus to avoid a downturn in the economy as overseas demand sank under the weight of the collapse in the mortgage market and a number of key Western financial institutions. The push by overseas companies into China funded a good portion of the growth in its factory sector, and the demand for cheaper production alternatives swelled the current account and allowed the sovereign wealth fund to balloon. This emboldened the government to double down on investment in many of the same industries where excess capacity was already evident.

Short-Term Performance Obsession

The transition from excess demand to excess supply is not just the result of the institutionalization and then the globalization of wealth; it is also a natural consequence of the way in which money managers are evaluated by investors and then compensated. A performance-driven investment culture has been a big factor contributing to the evolution of the broader macroeconomic environment we face today. The never-ending search for above-market/double-digit returns has steadily evolved into chasing money managers with the best short-term investment returns, and to an investment strategy based on quarterly earnings rather than discounted cash flow. The fascination of money managers with quarterly returns reflects the dynamic of a market dominated by professional money managers trying to maximize both the returns of their clients and their own compensation.

Financial theory clearly asserts that discounted cash flow is the correct model for valuing or choosing between different financial assets. But the uncertainty attached to estimating distant cash flows with any sense of confidence has led money managers to focus on a quarterly earnings target. Portfolio managers have much less information about a company's operations and future prospects than do company insiders, so these professional money managers tend to evaluate companies and their management based on their abilities to achieve short-term targets. CEOs and other corporate executives who are concerned about not just the health of the company but also their compensation, which is tied to the share price, reinforce the obsession with short-term performance and a quarterly earnings target. Quarterly earnings are also the short-term metric on which all companies can generally be contrasted for investment purposes.

Sizable stock price responses to earnings surprises suggest that short-term earnings, not long-term cash flow, drive stock prices. But whether stock prices respond to earnings announcements or the long-term implications of these announcements is unclear. Investors, on the other hand, see the stock price movement and naturally conclude that it reflects the earnings release, not the implications for long-term cash flows. Moreover, portfolio managers and equity analysts can easily be compared by their abilities to predict earnings changes more so than changes in discounted cash flows. The result has been a steady increase in equity market turnover as measured by the ratio of sales to portfolio value.

Between 1945 and 1964, for example, this measure of annual portfolio turnover averaged a steady 17%. This suggests that the average portfolio held a stock for about six years. Since then, however, the turnover rate has been on the rise, and portfolio managers now turn over their holdings by about 110% a year.

The average stock is now held for only about 11 months. If a 6-year holding period can be viewed as a long-term investment, then an 11-month holding period has to be viewed as speculating in stocks. This simple turnover rate has been criticized by a number of market participants as overstating the extent to which portfolio managers turn over their portfolio, resulting in a number of alternative measures being compiled; but the fact that short-termism has become an important discussion point among market watchers suggests there has been a shift in focus toward a very short, three-month performance-driven culture.

Inflation vs. Credit Cycles

The supply-side policies implemented by President Reagan, and the rapidly rising exchange value of the dollar brought about by the Volcker anti-inflation monetary policy, led to a shift in the balance in the economy away from excess demand in the 1980s. The institutionalized and globalized wealth, which began at the same time, provided the grease that made the transition to excess supply a seamless process. This fundamental shift in the economy began to show through during the recovery from the 1990 recession. Rather than the typical rebound experienced after each of the prior postwar recessions, the 1991 recovery was unique in that the jobless rate actually increased as the pace of activity increased.

The atypical nature of the recovery was the result of damage done to the balance sheets of financial institutions, and these took an extended period to correct. The financial headwinds confronted by the economy served to dampen the pace of recovery. Although some sort of financial disruption was associated with each prior business cycle, they were all precipitated by Federal Reserve efforts to control inflation, which caught one or two institutions by surprise. For the 1990–1991 contraction, that triggered a collapse in the thrift industry.

The fact that a credit problem played a key role in causing the downturn signaled that the balance between supply and demand, which had been skewed toward excess demand, was starting to swing toward excess supply. This transition would be pushed further along by the digital revolution, foreign trade, and the emergence of China as a manufacturing powerhouse. This fundamental shift in the economy is still not fully accepted by policy makers, even though deflation has emerged as an important threat to the economy in the years following the 2007 financial crises. The early signs of

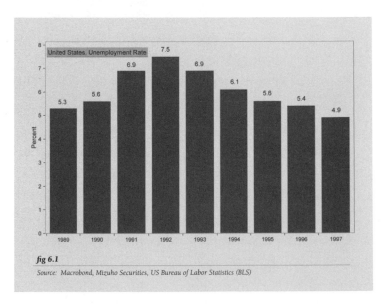

fig 6.1

Source: Macrobond, Mizuho Securities, US Bureau of Labor Statistics (BLS)

this transition go as far back as the mid-1980s and the collapse of the thrift industry.

S&L and Banking Crises of 1990–1991

The economy entered the 1990–1991 downturn in the usual manner. The Fed began tightening monetary policy in March 1988 to counter accumulating inflationary pressures. Cumulatively, the funds rate was increased from 6.5% to a high of 9.75% in February 1989, and it held there through May of the same year. The resulting recession, however, was anything but typical. Even though most Fed tightening cycles led to some sort of a financial accident, the 1988–1989 tightening cycle was preceded by credit-related turbulence that had not been seen since the Great Depression. Specifically, a run on Ohio thrifts by depositors forced regulators to temporarily close all savings and loan institutions in the state in an effort to ease insolvency concerns. The lines outside Ohio thrifts were not an isolated development. A couple of months later, in May 1985, Governor Harry R. Hughes of Maryland used emergency powers to limit depositor withdrawals from savings and loan associations to just $1,000 a month to avoid runs on institutions in the state.

The shock of seeing depositors line up outside financial institutions as they had during the Great Depression rocked the economy and financial regulators to their foundations. Aggressive lending to developers was amplified in Texas with the boom and bust in oil prices experienced during the 1980s. This caused a sharp local recession in Texas in 1986. Furthermore, the reduction in the tax advantage of real estate depreciation contained in the 1986 Tax Reform Act negatively affected heavily leveraged developers. Between 1986 and 1995 a total of 1,043 savings and loans were closed—one-third of all such financial institutions. The problem confronting thrifts at the time was an inherent mismatch between the short-term nature of their deposit liabilities, the fixed-rate long-term nature of their mortgage assets, and an inverted yield curve. The inverted yield curve and regulatory forbearance granted by politicians to keep the housing market thriving led to poor economic decisions and excessive development. By the time the S&L crisis unfolded, the housing market was completely out of balance, and the process of resolving the situation stretched out until 1995.

SHADES OF THE GREAT DEPRESSION

The collapse of the thrift industry brought back images of depositors waiting in long lines outside financial institutions to withdraw money in the wake of growing solvency concerns. A bank holiday and even a rationing of withdrawals were ordered to stop a run on these financial institutions, especially state-chartered institutions. The S&L crisis spilled over into a broader banking industry crisis, and, as a result, the 1990–1991 recession was the first of the credit-driven cycles of the postwar period.

Investors would subsequently learn that this was not a one-time development. Credit cycles, in fact, would cause the next two business cycles of the postwar period. The S&L crisis resulted in the failure of a full one-third of the 3,234 thrifts in existence between 1986 and 1995. The crisis would lead to the demise of the Federal Savings and Loan Insurance Corporation (FSLIC) and the establishment of a special-purpose vehicle designed simply to resolve failed thrifts—the Resolution Trust Corporation (RTC). The crisis would also cost the government an estimated $160 billion, making it the largest bailout recorded to that point. The primary drivers of the crisis can be lumped into four major categories, most of which showed up again as drivers of each of the next two business/credit cycles:

Macroeconomics

The 1970s proved to be a particularly difficult period for thrifts. Rising energy prices led to accelerated obsolescence of much of the country's capital stock, resulting in an unsustainable macro environment of rising inflation and joblessness. Stagflation would lead to rising short-term rates as the Fed tightened to curb inflation, further weakening the economy and eventually causing a recession. The short but deep Carter

"Credit Control"–induced recession of 1980 was followed very quickly by Volcker's shift to money supply targeting, leading to the first back-to-back recessions of the postwar period. This combination of economic stress and an inverted yield curve stressed the S&Ls, which were inherently mismatched between their assets and liabilities.

Deregulation

Congress deregulated the thrift industry through the passage of both the Depository Institution Deregulation and Monetary Control Act of 1980 and the Garn–St. Germain Depository Institutions Act of 1982. These two pieces of legislation allowed thrifts to offer a wide array of savings accounts and to expand their lending capabilities. Most important, this legislation reduced regulatory oversight of these entities. These changes were intended to allow S&Ls to grow out of the problems that stagflation and rising rates were causing. Other changes included authorizing more lenient accounting rules to report their financial condition and eliminating restrictions on the minimum number of shareholders.

Forbearance

As losses at thrifts mounted, regulators allowed insolvent institutions to remain open for political reasons—in part because S&Ls were viewed as critical to the housing market. The net result was an increase in imprudent lending. Once the government allowed insolvent institutions to continue to operate, management teams were incentivized to take on more risk in the hope that the developments they were funding would pay off in a big way and return the institution to financial health. This led to a mispricing of risk, and the result was a higher rate of default than expected. Essentially, S&Ls lent more money than was prudent for projects they could not properly evaluate.

Brokered Deposits

As part of the deregulation of the thrift industry, the 5% cap on CDs issued by thrifts was lifted. This allowed even a small S&L to raise a lot of money quickly simply by paying a somewhat higher rate of interest. To make a spread, the S&Ls had to invest in riskier assets. Brokered deposits inevitably led to a scam known as "linked financing" in which deposit brokers would steer large deposits to a thrift with the expectation that the thrift would subsequently make loans to predetermined borrowers.

The weakening of the thrift industry in the second half of the decade set the stage for a significant push into commercial real estate lending that would eventually impair the balance sheets of the banking industry, resulting in the first credit cycle of the postwar period. Although the role that balance sheet deterioration played in triggering the recession was largely unrecognized at the time, its effect on the jobless recovery rate started to show. Fed Chairman Alan Greenspan attributed the sluggishness of the 1991–1993 recovery to financial "headwinds" generated by the "constriction of credit in response to major losses at banks associated with real estate lending and foreign lending, coupled with a crisis in the savings and loan industry."

The overbuilding of commercial and multi-family real estate in the 1980s was excessive even for this highly cyclical industry. Commercial construction more than doubled in value between 1979 and 1985. Although there were clearly macro drivers behind this expansion, commercial construction climbed from 1.3% to 2.0% of nominal GDP over this six-year period. Economic and demographic factors increased the demand for commercial space and multi-family housing in the late 1970s and early 1980s. Employment growth accelerated as baby boomers continued to flood into the workforce and the participation rate of women rose. The economy was also shifting from manufacturing to a greater service orientation, leading to a 4% annual rise in office workers during this period, according to the FDIC.

Strong growth demand for office space was a key factor behind the boom in commercial construction and eventually in the overbuilding. The energy price gains in the late 1970s and early 1980s also boosted demand for commercial space in Texas and Oklahoma. The tumble in oil prices later in the

Year	Commercial Construction Spending (current dollars)	Commercial Construction as Share of GDP (% of nominal GDP)	Office Vacancy Rate (%)	Multi-Family Housing Permits (000s)
1979	33.5	1.3	5.2	444.8
1980	41.0	1.5	3.4	365.7
1981	48.3	1.5	3.8	319.4
1982	55.8	1.7	5.5	365.8
1983	55.8	1.6	10.8	570.1
1984	70.6	1.8	13.1	616.8
1985	84.1	2.0	15.4	656.6
1986	80.9	1.8	16.5	583.5
1987	80.8	1.7	16.3	421.1
1988	86.3	1.7	16.3	386.1
1989	88.3	1.6	16.1	339.8
1990	87.5	1.5	16.7	262.6
1991	68.9	1.1	17.4	152.1
1992	64.5	1.0	18.8	138.4

fig 6.2

Source: *US Bureau of Economic Analysis, Coldwell Banker vacancy rates from Hester (p. 127);
US Census Bureau (2008); Federal Reserve Bank of Kansas City, Q3 2008 Review.*

decade caught developers by surprise and resulted in regional overbuilding. The Reagan defense buildup and growth of the fledgling personal computer industry lifted the demand for commercial and residential development on the West Coast and in the Northeast. The biggest contributor to the boom, and then the bust (which crushed many banks), was the changes in the tax laws. The ERTA passed in 1981 lowered personal and capital gains tax rates but also introduced accelerated depreciation. These changes lifted the after-tax return on commercial projects, encouraging development. The ballooning budget deficits and the lessons learned from the collapse of the thrift industry caused policy makers in 1986 to reverse directions on depreciation and eliminated the ability to use passive losses against active income. A rapidly rising vacancy rate, especially in office space, further contributed to the construction bust of the late 1980s and early 1990s. Risk-based capital standards were also being phased in, which increased the costs to banks and borrowers and amplified the credit squeeze developers were facing.

The overbuilding left banks heavily exposed to non performing loans as the economy slowed and property prices fell in a rising vacancy environment. Banks had also become more aggressive in the wake of regulatory changes and the need to grow earnings. Commercial and real estate loans typically generated large upfront fees that went straight to the bottom line. Between 1980 and 1990, FDIC data shows that total loans and leases at insured banks increased to 63% from 55% of total assets, an 8% jump. Total real estate lending jumped from 18% to 27% of assets. To put this in perspective, it has been reported that bank loans and leases outstanding jumped

Year	1980	1990
Real Estate Loans	17.8%	27.1%
Commercial and Industrial Loans	19.5%	17.1%
Consumer Loans	9.6%	11.3%
Total Loans and Leases	**55.4%**	**62.8%**

fig 6.3a

Source: Federal Reserve Bank of Kansas City, Q3 2008 Review

from $1 trillion over this ten-year period to $2.1 trillion, while real estate loans tripled to $830 million and commercial real estate loans increased fourfold to $238 million. This exposure became a big problem as the real estate market deteriorated in the wake of overbuilding and excessive speculation. Non-performing loan balances rose from 3.1% to 5.2% of all loans and leases between 1984 and 1991. Net charge-offs jumped to 1.6% from 0.7%, but in commercial real estate, nonperforming loans rose to 8.2% and charge-offs increased to 2.1%.

Many of the banks that failed during this period were those that participated heavily in regional real estate booms. Of the banks that failed, for example, the average institution increased its real estate portfolio to about 30% from just about 6% of assets. On average, those that survived increased their portfolio weighting by about 5% to 11% of total assets. As

Year	Nonperforming Loans/ Total Loans*	Net Charge-offs/ Total Loans
1984	3.1%	0.7%
1985	2.9%	0.8%
1986	3.1%	0.9%
1987	3.7%	0.8%
1988	3.3%	0.9%
1989	3.6%	1.1%
1990	4.8%	1.4%
1991	5.2%	1.6%
1992	4.4%	1.3%
1993	2.8%	0.8%
1994	1.8%	0.5%

fig 6.3b

Source: *Federal Reserve Bank of Kansas City, Q3 2008 Review*

Year	Nonperforming Loans/ Total Loans*	Net Charge-offs/ Total Loans
1984	3.1%	0.7%
1985	2.9%	0.8%
1986	3.1%	0.9%
1987	3.7%	0.8%
1988	3.3%	0.9%
1989	3.6%	1.1%
1990	4.8%	1.4%
1991	5.2%	1.6%
1992	4.4%	1.3%
1993	2.8%	0.8%
1994	1.8%	0.5%

Note: Data is not available for years before 1984

fig 6.3c

Source: *Federal Reserve Bank of Kansas City, Q3 2008 Review*

a result, total bank closings and assisted transactions surged from 10 insured institutions in 1979 to 534 in 1989.

The deterioration in the banking industry's balance sheet during the run-up to the 1990–1991 recession resulted in an economic recovery unlike any other experienced during the postwar period. Prior to 1991, the unemployment that accompanied an economic downturn would begin to reverse shortly after the recession reached its trough as companies recalled workers. In 1991, this cyclical rebound failed to materialize, and the economy entered its first jobless recovery. Although the contraction ended in March 1991, the jobless rate continued to rise until 1993 and did not return to its pre-recession level until 1997. Payroll employment growth, which typically would have risen by about 7% in the first two years of a recovery/expansion, rose by only 0.7% between March 1991 and March 1993. This was little more than one-tenth of its normal rebound.

Economists at the time credited the slow recovery in employment to the shallow nature of the recovery and the unexpected spike in labor productivity. Annual growth in non-farm business output during the two years of recovery was less than 40% of the 6.25% average experienced during the comparable period of the previous seven postwar recoveries. Labor productivity also accelerated over this period, rising at almost four times the rate economists assumed was the trend.

Most economists who study this period focus on the acceleration in productivity, which was clearly an important factor in the jobless recovery but, as a result, little attention is given to the role that the banking industry's restructuring had on the recovery process. Rather than the economy benefiting from pent-up demand created by the downturn, and the economy's inherent excess demand, the 1991 recovery was disappointingly shallow. The need to repair bank balance sheets restrained overall aggregate demand until the restructuring was complete.

It is interesting to note that the jobless recovery ended as soon as the banking industry's balance sheet restructuring was completed in 1993. This atypical recovery marks the first postwar business cycle recovery that was determined more by a credit problem than inflation—it would also not be the last. Our analysis suggests that the two subsequent postwar recessions and recoveries would be again driven by credit-oriented disturbances rather than inflation, as all prior cycles had been. This marks a major shift in the dynamic facing the economy, with excess demand and inflation cycles being replaced by excess supply and credit-driven contractions.

Corporate Balance Sheet–Inspired Recession

The second credit-driven business cycle of the postwar period was March–November 2001. This recession ended the longest expansion in the postwar period, which spanned ten years. The eight-month 2001 contraction was preceded by a modest 175 basis point inflation-induced Fed tightening cycle to 6.5% from 4.75%; however, this monetary policy tightening was too small to have caused the downturn in the economy. The causes of the recession are generally considered to be the bursting of the technology bubble and the events surrounding the September 11, 2001, terrorist attacks. The technology bubble began to deflate after the NASDAQ peaked at 5,132.52 on March 10, 2000; but the cause of the recession has generally been considered the damage done by 9/11 to the economy and financial markets.

However, our analysis instead suggests that the corporate sector balance sheet restructuring—that was precipitated by fraud and excessive leverage—actually led to the contraction in the economy. The collapse of Enron and WorldCom both played a major role in bringing about the recession as well as the shallow nature of the recovery. The Fed's aggressive response to the 1991 recession and the fiscal stimulus applied by Congress should have resulted in a much stronger recovery. Yet this recovery proved to be one of the weakest in the postwar period. The Fed cut rates by 475 basis points, to just 1.75%, while Congress enacted the massive George W. Bush tax cut, the Economic Growth and Tax Relief Reconciliation Act of 2001 (EGTRRA). The Joint Committee on Taxation estimates that EGTRRA cost the government $1.65 trillion in lost tax revenue over ten years, and/or provided a 1.5% boost to real GDP; yet the recovery was anemic by all measures. This clearly suggests that something had changed in the economy, and we see it as indicative of the shift to excess supply.

EGTRRA

The tax cut initiated by President George W. Bush in the wake of the 9/11 terrorist attacks reversed a significant proportion of the tax increase undertaken by the Clinton administration in its first year. The Bush tax cut lowered tax rates for individuals. When fully phased in by 2006, the cut created a new 10% bracket for single filers with taxable income up to $6,000, to $12,000 for joint filers, and to $10,000 for heads of household. The new 10% bracket was made retroactive, resulting in a refund check of $300 for individuals and $600 for couples. The 28%, 31%, and

36% brackets were all cut by 3%—to 25%, 29%, and 33%, respectively. The upper 39.6% bracket was cut to 35%. EGTRRA also repealed the phaseout of itemized deductions and personal exemptions by 2008. The child tax credit was doubled to $1,000 per child. The capital gains tax was lowered to 8% from 10% for those in the 15% bracket. The law lowered the marriage penalty by increasing the standard deduction and by widening the 15% tax bracket for joint returns. The child dependent care tax credit was increased by 25%. Estate and gift taxes were lowered, with the estate tax phased out by 2010. Retirement savings contributions were increased. IRA contributions were increased from $2,000 to $5,000, and 401(k) limits

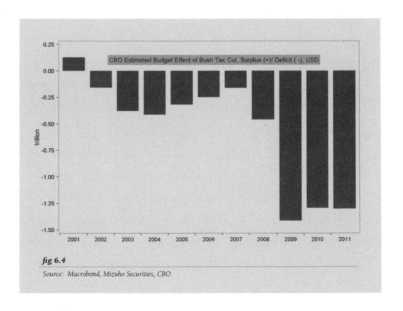

fig 6.4

Source: Macrobond, Mizuho Securities, CBO

bumped to $15,000. The bill also allowed a $4,000 minimum deduction for college tuition.

The recovery that followed in the wake of EGTRRA was decidedly sub-par, despite the aggressive nature of both the fiscal and monetary policy responses. This sluggishness was reminiscent of the jobless recovery of 1991–1993. Despite lasting just eight months, the contraction was unusually shallow. Real GDP declined by just 0.3% over the course of the three-quarter contraction in contrast to a 2% average decline. The loss in employment was also limited, at 0.7% less than the average. The rebound in both growth and employment after the economy bottomed out was also well below average, a development that our analysis suggests was the result of the nonfinancial corporate sector being constrained by the need to pay down debt, lengthen duration, and improve their credit ratings.

The failure of Enron caused the major rating agencies to rush downgrades, causing defaults to spike, especially in the independent power-producing space. As a result, investors reduced their risk tolerance and the economy/recovery suffered. More than one analyst at the time credited the rating agencies with having caused the recession. The result was a dramatic restructuring of corporate sector liabilities in an effort to calm investors' concerns. Corporate disclosure rules were tightened, and the relationships between Wall Street and investment banking clients were significantly altered under Sarbanes–Oxley. The Enron bankruptcy was followed by a number of other corporate failures such as the high-profile bankruptcy filing of Calpine after several years of struggling to overcome its financial problems. The need to pay down debt and lengthen maturities clearly dampened the *animal spirits* typically unleashed by aggressive policy actions.

Enron's primary business was the transmission and distribution of electricity and natural gas. The company built and operated power plants and pipelines. Enron owned a large network of natural gas pipelines that stretched from coast to coast and border to border, and it owned Northern Natural Gas, Florida Gas Transmission, and the Transwestern Pipeline Company. Enron was also involved in a partnership with Northern Border Pipeline of Canada. In addition to its domestic assets, Enron International focused on developing and building gas-fired power plants overseas, including those in Europe. Its Teesside plant in the UK was one of the world's largest gas power generation plants and provided 3% of the country's electric output. The Houston-based company also expanded into the water distribution business in Brazil, but that venture failed. Enron had a host of other investment projects in Europe, South America, Mexico, and the Caribbean. Despite the profitability of the international business, major power projects in India and in the Dominican Republic both failed miserably.

Under pressure to compete on a return basis with technology/growth companies that were attracting investors' interest, deregulation of the power industry in a number of states made independent power an alternative growth story. To boost the share price in order to finance growth, management began to use financial accounting to generate paper profits. According to regulators, Enron used a variety of "deceptive, bewildering, and fraudulent accounting gimmicks" to hide its losses. Essentially, management shifted liabilities to offshore special-purpose vehicles to shield the parent's balance sheet, creating the illusion of a healthy, vibrant company. In fact, Enron was named one of "America's Most Innovative Companies" by *Fortune* magazine six years in a row.

Despite repeated waves of investor concerns about its leverage, Enron was considered a blue-chip company and depended heavily on its ability to boost the stock price. To keep reporting strong profitability even as its finances deteriorated, Enron adopted mark-to-market accounting that allowed it to count anticipated future profits as current income. In other words, the financial health of the company became secondary to manipulating the stock price, according to comments made by former insiders. The company entered into complex financial transactions simply to boost current-period earnings, even at the expense of future profits. When the company eventually filed for bankruptcy after its share price collapsed in the wake of mounting investor concerns of fraud, it became apparent that management had also been involved in insider trading. The collapse of Enron shook investors' confidence and its auditor, Arthur Andersen, was discredited in the process. The sharp reduction in risk tolerance that followed prompted a

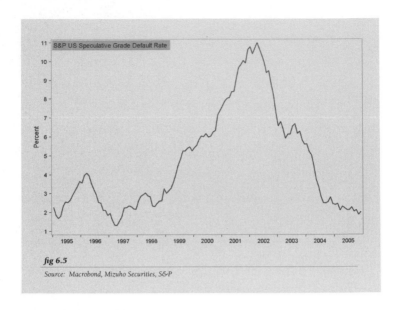

fig 6.5

Source: Macrobond, Mizuho Securities, S&P

spike in downgrades by the rating agencies. This forced the corporate sector to shift focus from growing their business to paying down debt, especially short-term debt that had been used for long-term investments. The result was a collapse in investment and earnings projections. This heightened sensitivity resulted in a spike in speculative-grade defaults that also dampened growth, as the peak in defaults did not occur until September 2002, almost a year after the trough.

Enron was not the only high-profile casualty during this period. Calpine was downgraded by Fitch in December 2001 to subprime, and this set in motion a chain of events that would eventually end in bankruptcy. Calpine was another independent power producer that tried to capitalize on the deregulation of the power industry.

Calpine had assets of $55 million in 1992 and was a

low-cost producer of electricity. Deregulation in California prompted management to add capacity, and the company bought natural gas production and other related businesses. Between 1998 and 2001, Calpine had compounded annual growth of 130% (assets) and 80% (capacity). In 1998 virtually all of its capacity was contracted, but by 2001 only 65% was sold forward. The remaining capacity was unhedged and dependent on open market conditions. The disruptions created by the Enron mess, a lack of weather-related demand, and Calpine's dependence on short-term funding led to forced asset sales in a failed attempt to remain solvent.

High-profile corporate failures were not confined to the independent power space. The telecommunication industry also experienced the largest default in history. WorldCom filed for bankruptcy protection in July 2002 after having reported in June that it had improperly accounted for $3.8 billion of expenses. This charge-off wiped out all of its profits for the five quarters, ending in the first quarter of 2002. WorldCom fueled its rapid growth through acquisition, and in the process accumulated $41 billion in debt. The rest of its funding was a combination of other short-term borrowing, including bank loans. This dependence on short-term borrowing proved to be its greatest weakness. Following admission of its accounting irregularities, many creditors pulled the plug on the company.

The problem at WorldCom began back in 1999 when businesses slashed spending on telecommunication services and equipment. The result was a sharp decline in the price WorldCom could charge in an environment of excess industry capacity. WorldCom had grown from a small long-distance company into a telecom giant through more than 60 acquisitions in just 15 years.

The demise of WorldCom followed on the heels of other scandal-ridden companies such as Tyco International, Global Crossing, and Adelphia Communications. These highly publicized failures not only rocked the equity markets, they also rattled the fixed-income and bank loan markets. This created problems for healthy companies as well, as investors turned defensive and management teams were distracted by the need to calm creditors' fears. The robust nature of the financial markets, along with the aggressive fiscal and monetary policies implemented after the bursting of the tech bubble and the attacks of 9/11, allowed the corporate sector to restructure rapidly, thus minimizing the depth of the downturn.

However, the shift to a more conservative management also limited the pace of the recovery. Growing excess supply problems were a key driver of the corporate sector's problems, as debt-fueled overexpansion ran head-on into declining prices, resulting in rising defaults—in other words, a credit/deflationary-induced cycle.

Double Trouble

The quick policy response to the corporate credit debacle that brought about the end of the technology bubble and led to the 2001 recession unwittingly set the stage for what would be the largest credit-driven recession since the Great Depression. The "Great Recession" would span 18 months—from December 2007 to June 2009—and would see the collapse of systemically important financial institutions such as Lehman Brothers and AIG, the forced mergers of Bear Stearns and Merrill Lynch, and the government conservatorship imposed on Fannie Mae and Freddie Mac. Investment companies Goldman Sachs and Morgan Stanley had to transform into banks to ensure their survival.

The credit cycle stretched overseas when Northern Rock, a medium-sized British bank, failed in September 2007, and it would prove to be the first of many such contagion-related failures that required foreign government rescue. The crisis hit a critical stage in September 2008 when IndyMac Bancorp filed for Chapter 7 bankruptcy protection and the commercial paper market began to collapse. A run on money market mutual funds began, as investors became worried that funds would "break the buck."

Investors scrambled to liquidate their investments. Withdrawals spiked to $144.5 billion during one week in September, up from just $7 billion the week before. This market disruption seriously interrupted the ability of domestic companies to roll over their short-term funding, which was used to support daily operations and fund payroll obligations. In response, the government had to extend insurance to money market mutual funds in order to stem the withdrawals, and the Fed had to establish a program to purchase commercial paper from mutual funds to ensure adequate liquidity. The financial market and economic disruptions that followed also involved the government takeover of General Motors after GMAC failed and the forced merger of Chrysler with Fiat. At the heart of the financial crisis were mortgage-backed securitized products and the derivatives investors used to hedge the risks imposed by these derivative securities.

The trigger for the Great Recession would be the collapse of the housing bubble, a bubble that had inflated home prices by 124% in the years between 1998 and 2006. During the two decades ending in 2001, home prices in the US ranged from 2.9 to 3.1 times median household income. This ratio rose to 4.0 times in 2004 and peaked at 4.6 times in 2006. Homeowners capitalized on this rise in value with the help of the banking industry and accumulated what would eventually be an unsustainable leverage ratio, even at exceptionally low interest rates. As with most credit cycles, the downturn was preceded by a series of Fed rate hikes from just 1% in 2004 to 5.25% in June 2006. The tightening was implemented by the Fed to contain anticipated inflation. The personal consumption expenditure deflator had bottomed out at 1.7% in January 2004 and climbed to a little more than 3% by August 2005.

In retrospect, I am sure the Fed would prefer to confront the limited inflation problems of the early 2000s, rather than the deflation risks the global economy struggles with today. Although the FOMC denies that its policy actions were designed to gradually deflate the housing bubble, their actions clearly played a role in what followed, especially through the adjustable-rate mortgage market. By September 2008, the average home price had declined by more than 20% from its mid-2006 peak. As prices declined, borrowers who were over-levered began to default—especially the flippers. This reinforced the decline in prices. Foreclosures subsequently rose, and by 2007 the total had risen to 1.3 million properties—a 79% increase over 2006. By 2008, this number expanded to 2.3 million properties or an 81% increase from 2007.

The collapse of the housing market destabilized the economy. Rather than these imbalances being highly concentrated in one or maybe two institutions, or in just one sector of the economy, this time the problem was spread broadly across the household sector *and* the banking industry. This was the first time since the Great Depression of the 1930s that the balance sheet problems were this far reaching, and the result would be a deep and protracted downturn followed by an uncharacteristically anemic recovery.

PLENTY OF BLAME TO GO AROUND

Many separate and complementary causes of the financial crises have been suggested by analysts. Although we cannot be certain which factors are to blame, the truth is that it was probably the result of all of these issues to some degree. According to the Financial Crisis Inquiry Committee, the crisis was caused by "widespread failure in financial regulation and supervision," "dramatic failures of corporate governance and risk management at many systemically important financial institutions," and "a combination of excessive borrowing, risky investments, and a lack of transparency by financial institutions."

Government inconsistency in policing markets has also been cited as a cause, as well as a reduction in mortgage lending standards. Deregulation of the over-the-counter derivatives market and the failure of credit-rating agencies to accurately price risk (given the increase in leverage added to the banking system), can also be listed as causes for the crisis. The repeal of the Glass–Steagall Act in 1999 that had separated banks and security firms since the Depression has also been cited as a cause. The growth of Alt-A, subprime, and no-document lending, as well as the push into adjustable rate mortgage products, can all be seen as the more immediate causes for the collapse in the housing market.

My assessment of the events focuses more on the role played by Fannie Mae and Freddie Mac, which eased lending standards while accumulating large portfolios of mortgages relative to the more traditional securitization and insurance roles of Fannie and Freddie. Rating agencies used dealer-derived models inappropriately to evaluate the risks implied by new derivative securities that were used to hedge the growing portfolios of mortgage-backed securities. Despite the push for increased lending under the Community Reinvestment Act (CRA) during the Clinton administration, which was intended to drive an increase in home ownership, and despite the second Bush administration's repeated attempts to rein in the GSEs on safety and soundness concerns—the GSEs were not reined in due to Congressional opposition. In the run-up to the financial crisis, estimates indicate that CRA- related lending increased to $4.5 trillion, and because the Federal Reserve viewed CRA loans as prime, there was a tendency for banks to make sub-prime CRA loans with upwards of a 3% higher interest rate. This increased lending contributed to the expansion in subprime lending preceding the crisis. Subprime lending accounted for just 8% of originations in 2004, but grew to 20% of the market by 2006; and fully 90% of these were adjustable rate mortgages.

The run-up in home prices also led to incredible growth in home equity lending by banks, something that also contributed to the crises. Estimates indicate that households extracted upward of $5 trillion over the 2001–2005 period, with $1.4 trillion extracted in 2005 alone. As a result, the rapid rise in home prices led to a dramatic increase in household leverage. Specifically, mortgage debt relative to GDP increased from 42% in the 1990s to 73% by 2008.

The active phase of the crisis began on August 9, 2007, when BNP Paribas bank terminated withdrawals from three company-sponsored hedge funds, citing "a complete evaporation of liquidity" in the financial markets. But the event that pushed the markets over

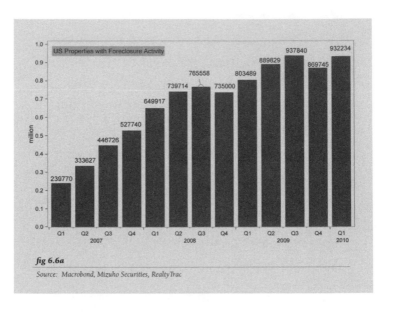

fig 6.6a

Source: Macrobond, Mizuho Securities, RealtyTrac

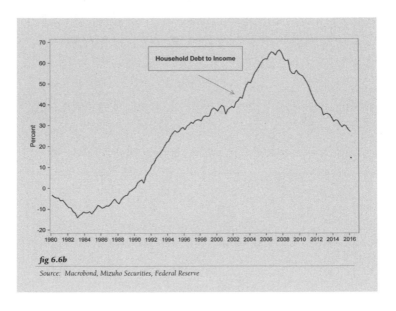

fig 6.6b

Source: Macrobond, Mizuho Securities, Federal Reserve

the edge was the September 8, 2008, announcement by Treasury Secretary Henry Paulson that the government was eliminating the dividend on the common and preferred stock of both Fannie and Freddie as part of the plan to rescue them. This shut off a key funding avenue for financial institutions in general, as the GSE conservatorship set a precedent as to how the government would deal with other failures.

The Great Recession pulled real GDP down by a record 4.2% as measured between its peak and trough. This contrasts to just a 1.9% average business cycle decline in real growth. Nonfarm payroll employment declined by 6.3% and industrial production plunged by 17.1%. The average decline for employment was only 2.7%, and for industrial production it was 8.8%. The civilian jobless rate spiked from a low of 4.4% to more than 10%, exceeded only by the 10.8% peak in joblessness experienced in the 1981 Volcker-induced recession.

The market dislocation spawned by the Great Recession of 2008 amplified the credit problems as the cause of the downturn. The Dow fell by almost 50% over the course of the downturn while the S&P 500 fell by 56.9%. The collapse in home prices and the tumble in equity markets crushed household wealth. Between June 2007 and November 2008, estimates show that households lost on average 25% of their collective wealth. The nature of the losses was concentrated in upper-income households. According to a Federal Reserve survey, 77% of the richest families saw a significant decline in wealth, while only 50% of households at the bottom of the pyramid suffered any decrease in their wealth.

This type of deep and extended decline should have resulted in a significant buildup in pent-up demand and a snapback in growth as the Fed rushed to ease policy in the wake of the collapse in activity. Instead, the recovery was unusually muted, and the expansion has been unusually shallow. These macro developments again attest to the unique effect that the double (household and banking system) balance sheet restructuring had on the economy.

One of the most obvious aspects of the unique nature of the current business cycle upturn is the decline in the labor force participation rate. This key labor market measure peaked at just under 51% in 2007 and has slid to under 49%, even as the economy turned upward. The improvement in the economy should have pulled discouraged workers back into the workforce, but that has not happened. In fact, the bulk of the decline in the jobless rate through the first couple of years of the recovery was the result of a declining participation rate rather than rising employment.

The other interesting aspect of the recovery/expansion that followed the financial crisis is that real GDP has tended to grow around 2% instead of the 3%–5% that typically occurs as pent-up demand is unleashed in the early stage of the recovery. In general, the recovery that began in July 2009 can be described as the second jobless recovery of the postwar period. This development has had a significant effect on monetary policy. Several years into the recovery/expansion, the Fed has yet to remove the majority of its policy accommodation, and no matter how much it has looked to reverse course, the fragility of the economy and the lack of inflation have stymied the Fed's intentions.

TRADITIONAL AND NONTRADITIONAL POLICY RESPONSES

The policy response to the financial crisis stretched over several years and included both fiscal and monetary initiatives. The first key piece of legislation was the Housing and Economic Recovery Act of 2008. This bill was signed into law by President George W. Bush on July 30, 2008, and expanded the government's regulatory authority over its GSEs, Fannie Mae and Freddie Mac. The bill also gave the Treasury authority to stabilize them by injecting liquidity if needed. The bill also raised the government's statutory debt limit by $800 billion to ensure adequate funding to meet GSE needs. As part of the Treasury conservatorship agreed to in September 2008, the Treasury injected $100 billion in capital into both Fannie and Freddie.

As the markets deteriorated in the wake of the GSE conservatorship agreement, the outgoing Bush administration, in concert with the top aide to the incoming Obama team, negotiated the American Recovery and Reinvestment Act of 2009, which was signed by President Obama within weeks of his being sworn in to office. The stimulus program was estimated to cost $787 billion but was later increased to $831 billion over ten years. Key provisions included the following:

- A new $400 per worker/$800 per couple tax credit for 2009 and 2010

- A one-year increase in the Alternative Minimum Tax floor, at a cost of $70 billion

- Extension of the child tax credit, even to families that did not make enough to pay taxes

- Expanded college tuition credit to $2,500 for 2009 and 2010

- $8,000 refund for all homes bought between January 1, 2009, and December 1, 2009

- $2,400 per person tax exclusion for unemployed workers

- Expanded earned income tax credit

- Expanded home energy tax credit

- Sales tax deduction for cars purchased, but phased out for families with incomes above $250,000

- Allowed companies to apply current losses against profits made over the previous five years

- $13 billion additional tax credit for renewable energy projects

- Bonus depreciation for companies through the end of 2009

In the wake of the financial market crisis, the Fed executed a series of supportive policies, beginning with a 50 basis point easing in late September 2007. This would be followed by several more rate reductions, which eventually pulled the target rate down to a 0.0%–0.25% range by December 2008. The FOMC also began paying interest on excess reserves in 2008

Round	Phase	Signaling or Announcement Date	Program Specifics
First (QE1)	1	November 25, 2008	• The Federal Reserve announces that it will purchase up to $500 billion of agency mortgage-backed securities (MBS) and $100 billion of federal-agency debt
		December 16, 2008	• The Federal Reserve first mentions the possible purchase of long-term Treasury securities
	2	March 18, 2009	• The Federal Reserve announces that it will purchase up to an additional $750 billion of agency MBS and increase its purchases of agency debt this year by up to $100 billion. Moreover, the FOMC decides to purchase up to $300 billion of long-term Treasury securities over the next six months
Second (QE2)		August 27, 2010	• Chairman Bernanke signals that the FOMC is likely to buy longer-term securities by saying it is one of the tools that the Federal Reserve retains for providing additional stimulus
	1	November 3, 2010	• The Federal Reserve announces that it will purchase a further $600 billion of longer-term Treasury securities by the end of 2011: Q2, at a pace of about $75 billion per month
Third (QE3)		August 31, 2012	• Chairman Bernanke states that the Federal Reserve will provide additional policy accommodation as needed to promote a stronger economic recovery and sustained improvement in labor market conditions in a context of price stability
	1	September 13, 2012	• The Federal Reserve announces an open-ended commitment to purchase $40 billion in agency mortgage-backed securities per month until the labor market improves substantially
	2	December 12, 2012	• The Federal Reserve adds a commitment to purchase $45 billion in longer-term Treasury securities per month

fig 6.7

Source: *Federal Reserve Bank of Cleveland, May 27, 2015*

when its implementation date was pulled forward from 2011 as part of the Emergency Economic Stabilization Act passed by Congress that year.

Nontraditional policy steps can be split into two separate categories: 1) targeted programs, and 2) large-scale asset purchases. The target programs included the Term Auction Facility (TAF), the Primary Dealer Credit Facility (PDCF), and the Term Securities Lending Facility (TSLF). The Fed also implemented a series of programs designed to provide liquidity directly to borrowers. These included the Commercial Paper Funding Facility (CPFF), the Asset-Backed Commercial Paper Money Market Mutual Fund Liquidity Facility (AMLF), the Money Market Investor Funding Facility (MMIFF), and the Term Asset-Backed Facility (TALF). The large-scale asset purchase programs were generally implemented in three waves and spanned a four-year period. The cumulative effect of these operations has increased the size of the System Open Market Account from under $1 trillion to well over $4 trillion. The Bernanke-led Fed began tapering its final wave of purchases beginning in December 2013.

This brief analysis of the past three business cycles strongly supports my contention that they were very different from prior postwar cycles. All three were dominated by a major adjustment in one or more of the economy's major macro balance sheet(s), and the Fed's role changed. In business cycles prior to 1990, the credit crunch was caused by the Fed's anti-inflation policies; and once the Fed's inflation objective was achieved, the economy came roaring back as policy was eased.

This reflected the Fed as leaning against the wind while the economy confronted excess demand. In each of the past three cycles, the Fed tightened rates in anticipation of a sustained rise in inflation; but in each case, the Fed tightening triggered a credit cycle that took on a life of its own. In every instance, the Fed had to deploy policy tools to smooth the balance sheet adjustment and assure that the downturn didn't become self-sustaining. This change in the nature of recessions reflects the economy's transition to excess supply. With inflation pressures limited, the length of expansions increased significantly relative to the average pre-1990 (postwar) business cycle. As such, the economy eventually became vulnerable due to balance sheet deterioration.

As leverage powered the economy, modest inflation pressures accumulated. The Fed eventually tightened monetary policy, causing a liquidity event that triggered the start of a new credit cycle. Because inflation never really took root, the unwind was quick, and inflation generally drifted lower as excess supply pushed tradable goods prices lower. Excess supply kept inflation from building in the late stages of the business cycle. The recession then pushed the long-term-trend inflation rate lower.

Measuring Macro Credit Quality

Business Cycles Have Become Credit Cycles

The transition from a world of excess demand to one of excess supply has fundamentally altered not only pricing dynamics in the economy, but also the basic nature of business cycles.

In essence, the economy now has the ability to grow at, or somewhat above, its long-term trend with very little risk of recession, unless one or more of the major macroeconomic balance sheets deteriorates to the point that a shock or liquidity squeeze becomes a full-blown credit crunch. Excess supply keeps inflation largely under control, which allows credit imbalances to build to the point where even a modest liquidity squeeze or exogenous shock can cause a full-blown credit crunch to take hold and trigger a contraction. Credit cycles (excess supply) are different from inflation cycles (excess demand) in that the initial liquidity squeeze expands into a broad-based economic disruption. In an inflation cycle, the initial liquidity squeeze may trigger a one-off credit event. But these are simply isolated incidents, and once the flow of liquidity is reestablished, the economy comes roaring back. The ability to snap back quickly reflects excess demand in the economy. In a credit cycle, the initial liquidity squeeze triggers a cascading effect that eventually involves many, if not most, of the participants in a key sector or industry.

Business cycles prior to the 1990 cycle were the result of the Fed's disintermediation of the banking industry by hiking short rates. The policy goal was to reverse an inflation trend that had emerged as a result of demand outstripping supply. However, the 1991 recovery was the first jobless recovery. The Fed's tightening resulted in much more than a simple disintermediation of the banking industry. Instead, it triggered a massive banking industry restructuring, which took years to correct. The lack of inflation pressures during the 1991–2001 economic expansion allowed the development of the next credit problem, this time in corporate balance sheets. Companies struggling to attain double-digit earnings growth in a world of tame inflation stretched their balance sheets to create the illusion of growth. This downturn was triggered by a series of corporate failures that resulted in a lack of credit flowing to the nonfinancial corporate sector. The necessary corporate balance sheet restructuring occurred in record time with the help of both fiscal and monetary policy stimulus designed to limit the damage to the economy from the 9/11 terrorist attacks. The absence of inflation also increased the willingness of the Fed to hold short rates very low, further facilitating the corporate restructuring. The shift toward excess supply was evident in the inflation data as corporate pricing power clearly diminished, but this was unrealized at that time.

With banks and households largely unscathed by the corporate sector restructuring of 2001, the stage was set for the next credit imbalance to form. This time the problems would surface in household balance sheets and extend to the banking industry. Eventually an accelerating global economy, powered by double-digit growth in China, threatened a rise in inflation; and the Fed again tightened. This tightening cycle caught the housing market in the midst of a speculative price bubble fueled by adjustable rate mortgage lending and a significant reduction in lending standards. The result was a forced household balance sheet restructuring and a massive consolidation in the banking industry that had loaned excessively to households. The complex financial innovations used to keep the housing bubble going even after the Fed started to raise rates eventually left the securities and banking industries, automotive industry, two government-sponsored enterprises, and a major insurance company all floundering. This credit super cycle has become known as the *Great Recession*.

From this perspective, it is clear that the ability of the economy to handle temporary liquidity squeezes is directly proportional to the health of the household, nonfinancial corporate, and banking industry balance sheets. An economy can handle exogenous shocks and/or Fed-induced temporary liquidity squeezes if balance sheets are healthy. Examples of such events are the Tequila Crisis of 1994, the Russian Debacle of 1998, and the failure of Long-Term Capital Management (LTCM) in the same year. Alternatively, if conditions are right even a modest shock or liquidity squeeze can cause a deep, prolonged downturn and a sub-par recovery in its wake. The length and depth of the downturn, as well as the strength of the recovery, are contingent upon the extent of the credit problem that needs to be corrected and the time required to restructure. This pattern suggests that the post-1990 business cycle turning points depend more on macro-credit quality than on inflationary pressures. The desire for double-digit returns in a world of low-single-digit inflation provides the motivation for an eventual deterioration in credit quality. Investors and corporations reach beyond their comfort levels to achieve returns that are increasingly difficult to obtain.

Why Reinvent the Wheel?

To gain insight into how best to measure macro credit quality, a basic understanding of how credit is assessed at the micro or individual level is useful. Data limitations also need to be considered, since most macro data are designed to help calculate quarterly GDP, not to assess balance sheets in a credit-scoring exercise. Fortunately, a very simple approach to measuring credit risk at the macro level appears to yield useful and exploitable information that both investors and policymakers can use.

Specifically, to assess macroeconomic credit quality, the economy can be broken down into four basic sectors: 1) the government sector; 2) the banking sector; 3) the nonfinancial corporate sector; and 4) the household sector. Each of these major credit buckets needs to be evaluated individually for its risk of default. This risk assessment is different from the event that actually triggers the recession, in that it provides a measure of the probability that a shock or liquidity squeeze would evolve into a full-blown contraction. The weaker the macro balance sheets, the higher the risk of a recession. The longer it takes to restructure after a disruption, the weaker the recovery process and the more stimulus needed to ensure the recovery continues until the adjustment is complete.

The *government sector* is the easiest to assess in that its ability to tax, and the relatively high domestic compliance rate among taxpayers, ensure that this sector will remain an investment-grade credit, unless policymakers increase the risk of default to further some political purpose. Examples of this are the debt limit showdowns that have surfaced periodically between Congress and different administrations over conflicting domestic policy agendas. Thankfully, all of these situations have been resolved before a default has actually occurred. This allows us to assume that the US government does not need a credit quality assessment. For many other countries this may not be the case, however, especially in emerging markets or less developed economies where government risk remains an important consideration.

CREDIT RISKS OF SOVEREIGN GOVERNMENTS

Sovereign Credit Risk is generally thought of as the risk of a government not being willing or able to meet its loan or debt obligations, or reneging on its debt guarantees. Five macro variables are generally thought to influence the ability of a government to repay its debtors: 1) debt service ratio; 2) export ratio; 3) investment ratio; 4) variance of export revenue; and 5) domestic money supply growth.

Sovereign defaults have tended to involve short-term foreign currency debt; as a result, there has traditionally been an emphasis on export revenue as the primary source of foreign currency reserves, which increases the government's ability to deal with liquidity crises. In addition to the macro variables above, the ratio of foreign currency reserves to short-term debt (especially short-term foreign currency debt) is also a source of reserves that are the first line of defense during a crisis. Many crises, known as "balance of payments crises," start with a large current account deficit that requires a continued flow of liquidity from overseas investors. A squeeze on a country's ability to roll over its debt, perhaps in the wake of a ratings downgrade, can cause these overseas flows to dry up. Alternatively, if the currency weakens, the foreign currency debt burden multiplies, and foreign currency reserves need to be deployed to stave off a default.

Faced with either of these situations, the economy initially contracts sharply as the funding from abroad slows, then recovers over the next few years as the weaker currency, which then helps exports become more competitive. A current account deficit larger than 5% of GDP is often seen as a warning sign. Interestingly, the US is often considered less susceptible to balance of payments crises, as the reserve currency status of the US dollar ensures demand, thus ensuring sustained funding from abroad.

It is important to mention that no financial institution in a country or region can have a credit rating higher

Ramp Category	Key Risk Factors	Key Comparator Variables
Political Stability	Political event risk	—
Economic Prospects I: Structure	Economic prosperity, diversity and resilience	• Nominal US$ GDP per capita
Economic Prospects I: Growth	Economic growth trends	• Growth of real local currency GDP per capita
Fiscal Flexibility I: Revenue, expenditure and balance performance	Budgetary flexibility	• General government fiscal balance/GDP
Fiscal Flexibility II: Debt and interest burdens	Strength of government balance sheet	• General government net debt/GDP • General government gross interest payments/gross revenue
Fiscal Flexibility III: Off-budget and contingent liabilities	Unreported and contingent claims on sovereign balance sheet	• Estimated off-budget and contingent liabilities/GDP
Monetary Stability	Sustainability of monetary and exchange rate policies	• Core inflation
External Flexibility I: Liquidity	Reserves adequacy and market access	• Gross external financing requirement/gross usable reserves
External Flexibility II: Public sector net external debt	Strength of public sector external balance sheet	• Public sector net external debt/current account receipts
External Flexibility III: Bank and private sector net external debt	Strength of financial system and nonfinancial private sector external balance sheets	• Financial system net external debt/current account receipts • Nonfinancial private sector net external debt/current account receipts

fig 7.1

Source: *Standard & Poor's*

than its sovereign. This makes sense in that most banks hold substantial government debt as capital. Recent examples of sovereign credit crises that had serious effects on financial markets include the Asian Crisis of 1997, the Russian Crisis of 1998, the Eurobond default by Pakistan in 1999, the Argentina crisis of 2001–2002, and the Uruguay financial turmoil of 2002. The most recent and largest was the European Sovereign Crisis that has embroiled Greece, Italy, Spain, and Portugal repeatedly since 2009. Because of the growing importance and frequency of these sovereign credit disruptions, the rating agencies have imposed more discipline on their government ratings process. An example of this can be found in fig. 7.1, which summarizes the S&P's process established in 2002.

A straightforward *banking industry* model consists of just two key indicators that reflect the financial health of this key industry. Banks are central to the economy's health in that they are the only entities in the economy that can either amplify or dampen monetary policy decisions through their decisions on lending. When banks are healthy and the Fed eases, the increase in liquidity provided is immediately allowed to flow into the economy and economic growth responds. This was the typical state of the banking industry in all postwar recessions and recoveries prior to the 1990–1991 consolidation.

Alternatively, when banks are unhealthy and liquidity is constrained, banks immediately clamp down on lending, the economy contracts, and the recovery is constrained until the restructuring is complete. The 1990–1991 downturn is a good example of this process at work. This recession involved the collapse of the entire thrift industry, while the 2007–2009 recession was dominated by a broader banking industry consolidation. The risks accumulating in the banking industry prior to both of these downturns were evident in key industry-wide data, even though it was a Fed-induced liquidity squeeze that initiated the recession. The banking sector risks were evident in rising nonperforming loan balances and a declining banking industry coverage ratio. The coverage ratio measures the banking industry's reserves relative to their nonperforming loan balances. Luckily the Federal Deposit Insurance Company (FDIC) provides reliable summary data on all the covered banks.

Generally the banking industry's health is improving when nonperforming loan balances are low and declining relative to overall loans and leases outstanding, and reserves are high and rising. The two key threshold levels for both measures can be seen clearly in figure 7.2. Bank balance sheets are healthy when nonperforming loan balances are declining and approaching 1.25% of total loans and leases, and when the coverage ratio is rising and approaching one dollar of reserves for every dollar of nonperforming loans. The higher the percent of nonperforming loans and the lower the coverage ratio, the worse the situation is for the industry and the economy.

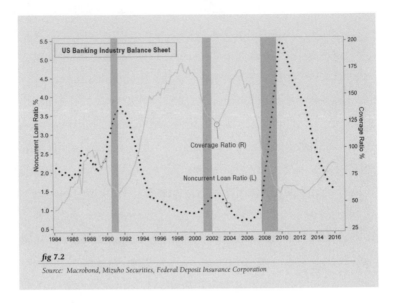

fig 7.2

Source: Macrobond, Mizuho Securities, Federal Deposit Insurance Corporation

Bank capital is also an important balance sheet indicator, but strict rules governing how much capital banks need to hold to support their lending have been imposed and may reduce the value of this measure going forward; in other words, higher capital ratios may mean that banks will be more conservative in their lending decisions.

Nonfinancial Corporate Sector

Corporate default risk is generally defined as the possibility that a corporation will be unable to meet required payments on debt obligations. Lenders and investors are exposed to default risk in virtually all forms of credit extension to the corporate sector. To compensate for the risk of default, lenders charge higher interest rates based on the perceived riskiness of the loan or investment. Default risk can be influenced by general macroeconomic conditions and/or an individual borrower's financial position. Essentially, anything that can influence a borrower's ability to make interest and principal payments affects their default risk.

Two important corporate statistics used to assess default or credit risk are free cash flow and the interest coverage ratio. Free cash flow is the cash generated after a company makes necessary internal investments and is calculated by subtracting capital expenditures from operating cash flow. Free cash flow is used, for example, for share repurchases and dividend payments. The interest coverage ratio is calculated by dividing a company's earnings before interest and taxes (EBIT) by its periodic interest payments—the higher this ratio, the healthier the company. Statistical analysis conducted by the Federal Reserve Bank of New York in 1994 suggested that the spread charged on a triple-A ("AAA") debt issuer over a comparable long-maturity Treasury obligation will be about 43 basis points. A triple-C ("CCC") corporate issuer would need to pay an extra 724 basis points. This analysis highlights how important credit risk considerations are to both the borrower and the lenders.

There are three principal rating agencies—Moody's, S&P, and Fitch—and all use a simple letter system to rank relative credit risk.

Financial Risk Profile (ie. Leverage)						
Indicative Ratios	**Minimal**	**Modest**	**Intermediate**	**Significant**	**Aggressive**	**Highly Leveraged**
FFO*/Debt (%)	greater than 60	45-60	30-45	20-30	12-20	less than 12
Debt/EBITDA (x)	less than 1.5	1.5-2.0	2-3	3-4	4-5	greater than 5
Debt/Capital** (%)	less than 25	25-35	35-45	45-50	50-60	greater than 60
Excellent	AAA/AA+	AA	A	A-	BBB	--
Strong	AA	A	A-	BBB	BB	BB-
Satisfactory	A-	BBB+	BBB	BB+	BB-	B+
Fair	--	BBB-	BB+	BB	BB-	B
Weak	--	--	BB	BB-	B+	B-
Vulnerable	--	--	--	B+	B	B- or below

Business Risk Profile (left axis label)

fig 7.3

Source: Adapted from "Methodology: Business Risk/Financial Risk Matrix Expanded," Standard & Poor's, 2012

At the company level, the rating agencies look at many credit measures, some of which can be adapted to assessing the health of the sector in general. The three principal variables assessed in all corporate rating scores are a company's leverage ratio, duration structure, and debt burden. Generally, the more leveraged a company is, the shorter the duration of their borrowing; or, the higher the debt burden, the riskier the credit. By combining data available from the Federal Reserve's Flow of Funds (FF) and the Bureau of Economic Analysis (BEA) National Income and Product Accounts (NIPA), comparable measures can be calculated for the nonfinancial corporate sector. From the NIPA and FF data, we can calculate the net debt-to-sales ratio, which can be used to measure the degree of leverage in the nonfinancial sector. From the FF data, we can measure the relative level of short-term debt outstanding for the nonfinancial sector as a surrogate duration measure. And finally, the NIPA profits data provides reliable information on the nonfinancial sector's interest payments, and the interest-to-profits ratio will tell us the debt burden.

The weight assigned to each of these measures is also important in determining the sector's exposure to a liquidity squeeze or exogenous shock. For simplicity, an equal weighting yields a simple binary score of either improving or deteriorating credit quality by taking the ratio of the positive to negative indicators. Alternatively, doubling the weight given to the leverage ratio in this calculation yields a weighting scheme that allows for a neutral credit score falling somewhere between improving and deteriorating. Default rates should also be considered, but how much additional information they bring to the table is questionable.

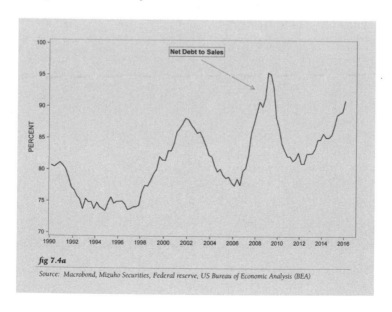

fig 7.4a

Source: Macrobond, Mizuho Securities, Federal reserve, US Bureau of Economic Analysis (BEA)

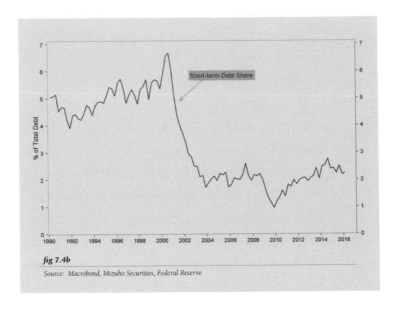

fig 7.4b

Source: Macrobond, Mizuho Securities, Federal Reserve

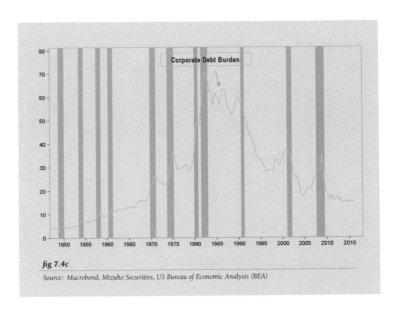

fig 7.4c

Source: Macrobond, Mizuho Securities, US Bureau of Economic Analysis (BEA)

Household balance sheets can be analyzed in a similar manner to that of the nonfinancial corporate sector, with some modifications to take into consideration: the differences in sources and stability of income and expenditures. The leverage ratio has to be modified from the corporate net debt to sales to the household's debt-to-income ratio.

To calculate this ratio, a combination of NIPA and FF data is used. To determine if this ratio is improving or deteriorating requires a simple comparison relative to its trend. However, a one-time adjustment has to be made for the advent of securitization that increased the debt load banks are comfortable with households carrying. FF data can also be used to calculate the household sector's duration structure, and the Federal Reserve calculates a household financial obligations ratio that can be used as a debt burden.

At the household level, the leverage ratio is probably the most important of the three measures, suggesting doubling its weight relative to the other two measures as discussed with regard to the score for the nonfinancial corporate space. Alternatively, default rates on many household credit products are available, but these do not give as good an idea of when and why balance sheets begin to deteriorate. Is it due to excessive borrowing, rising rates, or just a slowing economy?

Most lenders that service individuals or households look at FICO scores to determine the risk implied and to set the appropriate spread to charge. FICO is short for the original name of the company (Fair Isaac Company), and it is not a credit reporting agency. Rather, FICO uses data from the three

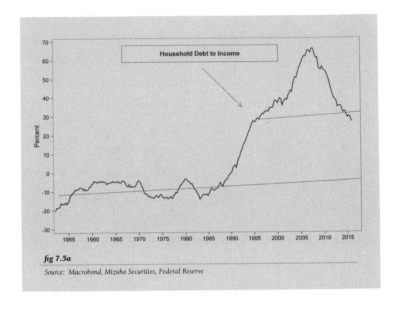

fig 7.5a

Source: Macrobond, Mizuho Securities, Federal Reserve

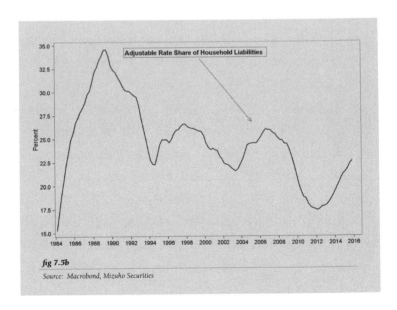

fig 7.5b

Source: Macrobond, Mizuho Securities

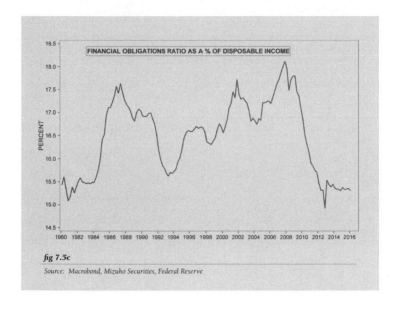

fig 7.5c

Source: Macrobond, Mizuho Securities, Federal Reserve

major agencies to develop its evaluation of lending risk. The three largest reporting agencies are Equifax, Experian, and TransUnion. FICO scores range between 300 and 850, with a higher score suggesting a lower risk of default. FICO scores are calculated from several areas of a person's credit report and different measures have different relative weightings depending on historical experience and behavior.

For the general population, the weights applied to the five major measures used to calculate a FICO score are as follows: 35% for payment history; 30% for amounts owed; 15% for length of credit history; 10% for credit mix; and 10% for new credit extensions. In general, a good payment history adds to a person's score; the amount owed is not always bad for the score but will tend to make it harder to improve the score; the length of someone's credit history is typically a positive; and a mix of credit is important. The more unsecured credit owed, the lower the score. The addition of new credit is often a negative; opening several new credit cards is viewed as a potential credit red flag.

The credit measures considered for major macro sectors are all on the liability side of their balance sheets. The Bank for International Settlements (BIS) has developed a useful data series they call "Total Credit" that encompasses all nonfinancial debt in a country—e.g., government debt, household debt, and nonfinancial corporate debt. The data include both domestic and external (owed to nonresidents) debt, including loans and debt securities; past data series did not consolidate these debts. The sovereign and financial crises of 2009 taught us that nongovernment debt sometimes becomes, in principle,

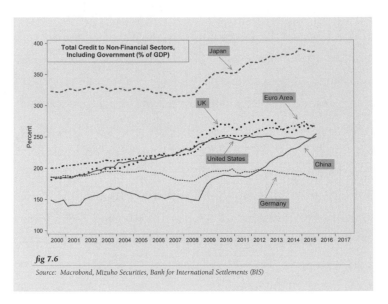

fig 7.6

Source: Macrobond, Mizuho Securities, Bank for International Settlements (BIS)

government debt as bailouts are conducted. In the US, household mortgage debt was essentially taken onto the federal balance sheet. Watching this measure could help the surveillance of credit bubbles; for example, China's debt is growing rapidly, led by nonfinancial corporate debt, while Japan's debt has been led by the government. Both China's nonfinancial corporate debt and Japan's government debt are now over 200% of GDP.

The asset side of balance sheets has been ignored in this analysis because cash flow and liquidity concerns are more important than the asset/liability ratio. Although assets can be liquidated to meet financial obligations, they are often not very liquid or are subjected to significant market volatility. As such, when trying to assess whether a liquidity squeeze or a shock will have either broad-based or just localized effects on the economy, cash flow is decidedly more important. It is important to recognize that asset-side considerations were used extensively to justify the accumulation of household mortgage debt in the run-up to the 2007–2009 recession.

Put simply, rising home values allowed borrowers to borrow more than they should have. When the housing bubble burst, however, the declining valuations made the situation worse, as many homeowners were left upside down on their mortgages and had an incentive to abandon or otherwise walk away from their homes. This explains why it is more important to look at cash-flow-based credit risk measures for households.

The same reasoning can be used for applying a similar measure for assessing the risks of a major credit disruption forming in either the banking industry or the nonfinancial

Disequilibrium

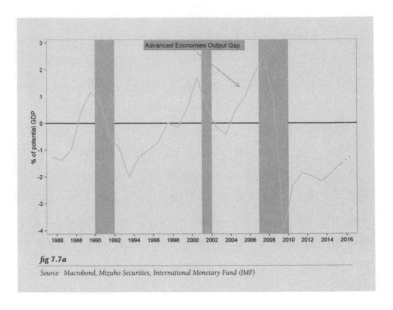

fig 7.7a

Source: Macrobond, Mizuho Securities, International Monetary Fund (IMF)

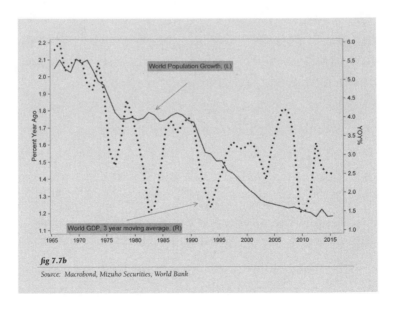

fig 7.7b

Source: Macrobond, Mizuho Securities, World Bank

corporate industry—the two major macro corporate credit sectors. The net implication of this risk-based assessment is that policymakers need to be much more vigilant in setting policy. Simply targeting inflation may have been the right thing to do in a world of excess demand, but it can lead to significant unintended consequences in a world of excess supply.

Pulling It All Together

The transition from inflation cycles to credit cycles reflects a fundamental shift in the domestic economy—and more important, the global economy—from a position of excess demand to that of excess supply. This move from one disequilibrium to another implies a radical new approach to analyzing business cycle risks as well as quantifying the nature of recoveries. This move also suggests that modern macroeconomic theory needs to be more focused on stimulating demand and creating jobs rather than fighting inflation. A Japan-like US output gap implies the existence of excess supply and/or lack of demand, and inflation is harder to generate.

This need to redress the focus of policy pertains not only to monetary policy but also to fiscal policy. Today's macroeconomic problems are more like those surrounding the Great Depression than those during the run-up to the Great Inflation of the 1960s to the early 1980s. Accepting the new imbalance

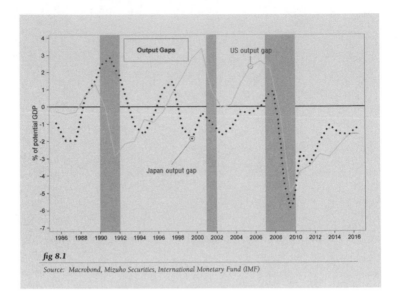

fig 8.1

Source: Macrobond, Mizuho Securities, International Monetary Fund (IMF)

between supply and demand as a given helps to explain both the difficulty Japan has had in exiting deflation and the ongoing battle Europe is waging to stave off deflation. It also helps to explain the demographic challenges confronting the developed world and the skewing of the income distribution that is proving to be a growing domestic problem.

Today's supply/demand disequilibrium reflects the natural response of policymakers, companies, and investors to the damaging effects of the Great Inflation. Essentially, the excess demand triggered by the end of WWII led to a period of rising inflation. The economic boom that followed the war created the middle class, the baby boom, the growth of the suburban lifestyle, and an increased social as well as environmental consciousness. These factors, when combined with the geopolitical aspects of the Cold War and the fiscal and monetary policy

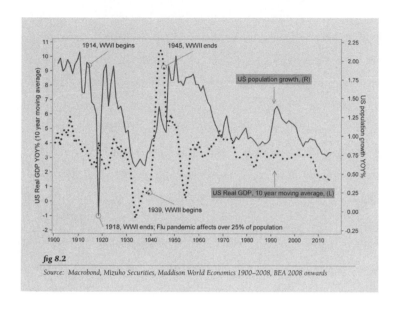

fig 8.2

Source: *Macrobond, Mizuho Securities, Maddison World Economics 1900–2008, BEA 2008 onwards*

framework that was developed to counter the Great Depression, resulted in an upward wage-price spiral—one that was amplified by the postwar strength of the labor unions. The rising interest rate environment and repeated inflation-induced recessions produced the stagflation of the late 1970s. This destructive macro environment sparked a shift in both monetary and fiscal policy that would have a profound effect on the economy, leading to the disequilibrium of excess supply and credit cycles that the economy now confronts.

Monetary policy was refocused from its previous focus on supporting fiscal policy decisions to instead aiming to control inflation. The Reagan supply-side revolution eventually succeeded in shifting the balance away from excess demand to excess supply. This shift in aggregate supply was the result not of lower taxes but of deregulation, the weakening of union power following the air traffic controllers' strike, the decline in long-term rates sparked by the Clinton tax hike, and the explosion of Al Gore's Internet.

At the same time, the high real returns that had evolved during the postwar period led to the institutionalization and globalization of wealth. These trends extended the period of above-normal returns in the postwar period to the point that double-digit return expectations became a given. This facilitated the shift away from defined-benefit to defined-contribution pension schemes, which pitted workers' interests against their own retirement needs. A natural consequence of these developments has also been the destructive shortening of investment horizons to today's three- to six-month window.

The need for double-digit returns on the three- to six-month basis that sparked the globalization of wealth and the

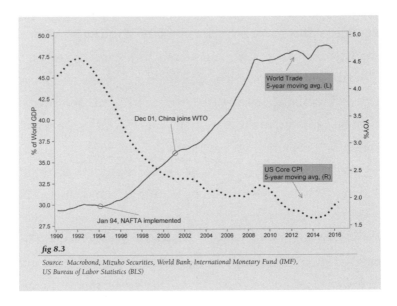

fig 8.3

Source: Macrobond, Mizuho Securities, World Bank, International Monetary Fund (IMF), US Bureau of Labor Statistics (BLS)

subsequent boom in emerging economies finally culminated in the boom in China as companies sought ever-cheaper sources in a world of declining inflation and high short-term rate expectations.

The shift from excess demand to excess supply altered the nature of the business cycle from simple inflation cycles to complex credit cycles. In inflation cycles, the economy has simply overheated in the wake of excess demand; while in a credit cycle, something goes fundamentally wrong and the workout period can be both very lengthy and quite costly. The need to restructure balance sheets also dampens the recovery phase of the business cycle, requiring longer periods of monetary stimulus after lower inflation has pulled down long-term rates. A flatter yield curve, when combined with the drive for double-digit short-term returns, leads to increased risk taking, which then sets the stage for the next credit cycle.

Policymakers have been slow in recognizing these changes in the economy. Their reliance on their interest rate–setting role over their regulatory responsibilities has resulted in investors incorrectly blaming the Fed for providing too much stimulus—when they have really been guilty of not exercising their regulatory oversight to control excessive risk taking. If the Fed had been paying closer attention to the expansion in mortgage lending in the run-up to the 2007–2009 recession and moved to temper the most aggressive of these new products being offered, the increase in risk being piled onto financial company balance sheets and the role the GSEs played could have been significantly reduced, if not avoided completely. As a result, near-zero interest rates, quantitative easing, and the need for overly restrictive new regulation would not have been necessary—let alone the recent talk of helicopter money.

Fiscal policy also has to change to address the transition from excess demand to excess supply and the unachievable drive created by the demand for double-digit short-term returns in a world of single-digit inflation, or worse, deflation. We need radical surgery to better align policy with the reality of excess supply. Policymakers must focus on stimulating demand and cultivating job growth in areas where technology has not replaced the need for workers. Clearly infrastructure, education, health care, and defense are areas where value-added comes from the people as well as the equipment. We also need to reduce the red tape that gets in the way of such spending, especially infrastructure spending. A much better balance has to be struck between growth and environmental concerns. Spending money on renewable energy should occur only if the downstream gains can be internalized domestically.

There are other aspects of fiscal policy that also need to be explored: Why do government workers have a union? Why do teachers have tenure? Should we eliminate all the government subsidy programs and consider providing one income safety net that offers a guaranteed minimum standard of living, including health care for all individuals and/or for the average family? This benefit would be unaffected by any increase in an individual's income above the set minimum, but any income above this level would be taxed. Individuals and households would then be responsible for obtaining all their own necessary goods and services—including housing and health care. The private sector would step in and provide quality services if the buyers had the means to pay for them and the courts recognized this in their decisions—and held individuals accountable to satisfy their obligations.

Tax policy also needs to be looked at in unique ways. The demand for high short-term returns could be altered by changing capital gains tax laws. Specifically, changing the current system for a system in which any gain recorded in less than five years would be taxed as ordinary income, while any gain after five years would be tax-free. This would alter corporate behavior and investment horizons—as well as return expectations—overnight.

Corporate taxes could be eliminated, but employers could be required to provide health care to all full-time and part-time employees. All corporate tax expenditures (e.g., corporate subsidies) could also be eliminated to reduce government's influence on the private sector. All medical insurance companies could be converted from for-profit businesses to mutual companies. This would better align the needs of those companies with those of its policyholders, not its shareholders. And outside the medical insurance area, mutual insurance companies would also take a more realistic approach to what they require from their policyholders in terms of compliance as well as settlements to avoid litigation.

Individual income tax policy also needs to be revamped to be more equitable. No one should get more out of the system than they put in, and the tax rates need to extend well beyond

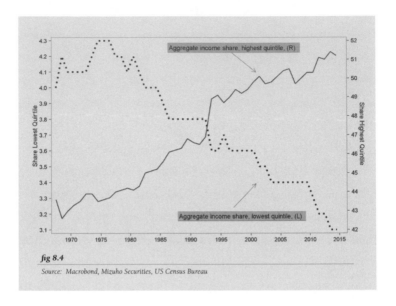

fig 8.4

Source: Macrobond, Mizuho Securities, US Census Bureau

today's 39.6% cap on top earners. The brackets also need to extend much further up the income ladder to reflect today's more highly skewed income distribution—an imbalance that leads to deeper problems such as lower population and/or lower economic growth. All other forms of income (excluding capital gains, as noted previously) could also be treated as ordinary income from a tax perspective. All deductions and exemptions could also be eliminated, except for state and local tax deductions, to reduce the distortions created by our tax laws and avoid double taxation. Sales taxes would also be deductible under this general concept.

In general, we need to recognize that the postwar world of excess demand is over, and, much as the world is struggling to find a new geopolitical balance, we need to look for a new macroeconomic framework as well. Thinking outside the box is called for because of the risk of deflation. We cannot count on today's service-oriented inflation to provide unlimited immunity from deflation. Whereas Japan has been struggling with deflation for 25 or more years, they actually started from a position of being the world's largest net creditor. On the other hand, the US is a large net debtor; and combating deflation may prove to be impossible should we fall victim to its embrace. If we look at Europe as a microcosm, we would unfortunately be in the positions occupied by Greece, Italy, or Spain, rather than that of Germany.

Two Sides of the Same Coin?

Secular stagnation and excess supply have a number of similarities, but they are fundamentally very different. Secular stagnation suggests that the economy suffers from an increased marginal propensity for individuals and households to save and a decreased propensity for companies to invest in new plants and equipment. The resulting imbalance between savings and investment drags down demand, reducing growth and inflation, and pulls down real rates. The secular stagnation camp suggests that an aging population and increased income inequality have contributed to the driving up of household savings, which reduces demand relative to supply. This demand shortfall subsequently reduces the need to invest, which limits the economy's potential growth rate as well. The application of fiscal policy is then suggested as the key to reversing this disequilibrium. This explanation is much like that put forward by Paul Krugman to correct his "liquidity trap" stimulus.

A key problem with secular stagnation is that households have not significantly increased their rate of savings; it has been the corporate sector that has increased its savings. In fact, the corporate sector is cash rich, which further weakens the secular stagnation argument. Companies have opted to build up their savings balances instead of investing in new plants and equipment because they see the return on investing their cash in financial assets and in their own stock as superior to the return they can get from building new plants and equipment. This contradicts the low real return argument, but is fully consistent with the idea that excess supply has lowered the return on investing in new plants and equipment due to a lack of pricing power through excess supply.

The excess supply explanation, on the other hand, suggests that the economy is suffering from a hangover in the wake of excessive investment spending in the post–Great Inflation period that pushed out the aggregate supply curve and subsequently dampened pricing power. This deflationary bias increases the incentive to save while reducing the need to invest. Saving tends to increase when individuals, households, and/or companies know they can buy more tomorrow than they can today. Household savings has not increased significantly, because the corporate sector has been laser-beam focused on achieving double-digit short-term returns in light of aggressive shareholder activism.

Excess supply suggests that there is less need to invest

as the global economy can already produce more goods than households can afford to consume without relying on excess leverage. As such, companies invest further only to cut their costs. Although current investment spending is reduced, prior over-investment leaves potential long-term growth unchanged. The excess investment in new capacity is seen as the direct result of investors seeking unrealistic, high short-term returns in a declining interest rate environment, resulting in a cost-cutting demand reduction spiral.

Excess supply also explains the growing income inequality problem and the growing pool of discouraged workers, which adds to the power of this explanation. Increased income inequality is the result of a substitution of capital for labor, which increases the returns to the owners of capital. Workers become discouraged when they cannot find work at a reasonable wage. The excess supply scenario calls for increasing demand to absorb the excess supply. This is not to be done by simply increasing government spending and leverage, but rather by increasing the after-tax return that companies can earn on human capital over physical capital—thus reversing a trend that has been in place since the early 1980s.

Appendix

Is the US Becoming Another Japan?

By Tetsuo Ishihara

The transition from excess demand to excess supply discussed in this book is primarily US focused; however, there are a number of similarities in the current US macro dynamic to that which Japan has confronted for more than a quarter century. The lesson learned from Japan is clear: Exiting deflation is much harder to accomplish than reversing an inflation cycle. More important, Japan has been able to deal with deflation for the past 30 years because it slipped into it from an enviable position—Japan was the largest net creditor nation. By contrast, the US is a large net debtor nation. Being heavily leveraged in a period of deflation makes paying back the debt substantially harder.

Although both countries followed very different paths to their current positions, it is important to recognize that both situations were created by a credit problem that involved both the banking industry and one of the other major macro balance sheets. Japan suffered a collapse in its highly leveraged commercial real estate sector between 1990 and 1991 that also severely damaged its banking industry. In the US, it was the housing bubble that burst and crippled the banking industry. The Bank of Japan (BOJ) and the Fed have both been forced to undertake alternative policy easing to try to reverse the damage. It can be argued that both central banks have had only limited success in their repeated attempts to stimulate their economies and stave off deflation.

Moreover, the same can be said for the dynamics unfolding in Europe and China. The broad-based nature of this problem supports this book's conclusion concerning the transition from inflation cycles to credit cycles and the link to an imbalance between aggregate supply and aggregate demand. Essentially, the shift is a global phenomenon, and because each region is politically and socially very different and entered this situation through different paths, the one-size-fits-all monetary policy prescription currently being employed has failed to deliver. To this end, we thought it would be useful to include a comparison of the Japanese and US experiences.

Similarities

Deterioration in the Quality of Available Job Opportunities

Although Japan continues to have one of the lowest unemployment rates of the industrialized world and the job-openings-to-applicants ratio in Japan has improved even more since Abenomics, job growth has been driven by low-wage jobs. For example, job growth in Japan in 2015 was led by the leisure and hospitality, health care and social assistance, and retail and wholesale sectors. Similarly, job growth in the US in 2015 was led by leisure and hospitality (e.g., fast food, waiters), education and health services (e.g., personal care aides), retail (e.g., retail outlet sales), and administrative and waste (e.g., temp staff, janitors). Many in Japan blame the deterioration in job quality on the multi-decade strengthening of the yen from around 250 JPY/USD in the 1980s to a disastrous strengthening of 75 JPY/USD in 2011. This caused a "hollowing out" of Japan's manufacturers due to a loss in export competitiveness. As a result, they moved factories and jobs abroad (sound familiar?). Abenomics is an attempt to weaken the yen in the hopes that manufacturers will return

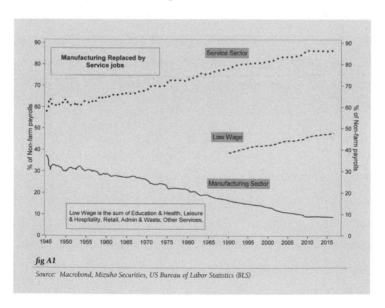

fig A1

Source: Macrobond, Mizuho Securities, US Bureau of Labor Statistics (BLS)

to Japan and return middle-class jobs. The US jobless rate has also declined sharply over the past few years to just under 5%, while the Job Openings and Labor Turnover Survey (JOLTS) data suggest that job openings continue to grow. However, as in Japan, the quality of jobs here in the US has been exceptionally disappointing and the loss of quality jobs to overseas has become a hot-button political issue.

Loan-to-Deposit Ratio Suggests No Desire to Lend

A key indicator of the demand for Japanese government bonds (JGBs) has been the loan-to-deposit ratio at banks. When banks cannot lend, they buy JGBs to earn a coupon on their deposit balances. Japan's experience and the BOJ's quantitative easing policies have steepened the yield curve, allowing banks to earn a spread between the interest they pay on deposits and the coupons they receive from their bonds. These earnings were then used to write down bad real estate debt. These policies, however, flattened the yield curve and slowed the restructuring process.

The collapse of the housing market in the US has had a similar effect on the demand for Treasury securities, and the loan-to-deposit ratio has also plunged. Banks have generally used their portfolio income to help repair their balance sheets. Central bank policies have also played a role in this process. Unlike the situation in Japan, US banks have tended to buy agency mortgages and to retain the mortgages they originate in order to generate the reserves necessary for restructuring.

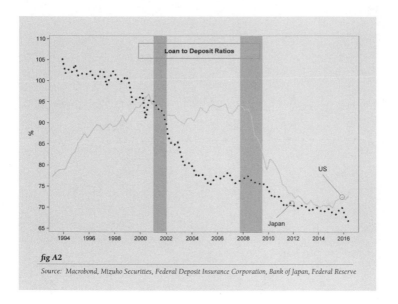

fig A2

Source: *Macrobond, Mizuho Securities, Federal Deposit Insurance Corporation, Bank of Japan, Federal Reserve*

Deflationary Pressures Evident in the Economy

Excess supply suggests a lack of corporate pricing power and a general downward pressure on prices. One important measure of excess supply is the output gap, or the difference between estimated potential GDP growth and actual GDP growth. A negative output gap implies an excess supply of goods and services and deflationary biases. Conservative estimates of the output gap published by institutions, such as the IMF, suggest that much of the developed world is facing an output gap; and Japan and the US are no exceptions. This clearly explains why companies remain focused on cost cutting and financially engineering earnings.

Disequilibrium

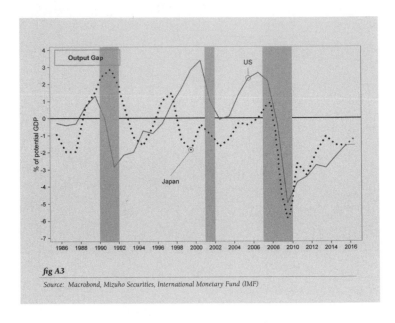

fig A3

Source: Macrobond, Mizuho Securities, International Monetary Fund (IMF)

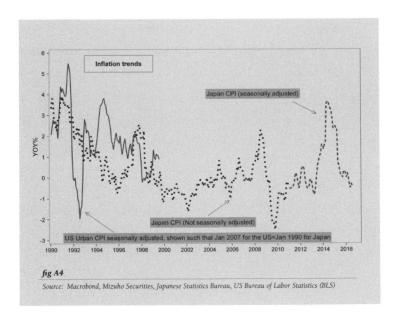

fig A4

Source: Macrobond, Mizuho Securities, Japanese Statistics Bureau, US Bureau of Labor Statistics (BLS)

Interest Rates Are Low at Both Ends of the Yield Curve

Low interest rates are another common factor experienced by both the US and Japan. After decades of zero or near-zero rates, the BOJ's move to negative interest rates in 2016 has prompted speculation that the US could be next. In Japan the move to negative short rates has caused a panic among senior citizens, even though they were not applied to retail deposit rates. For example, immediately after the policy shift, home safes sold out at home improvement stores where advertising displays read, "Are you ready for negative interest rates? Buy your fire-proof safe now!" Many individuals and households assumed it would not be long before negative retail deposit rates would be imposed. Interestingly, negative rates did not spur consumption as the BOJ had hoped; instead, it suppressed household spending. Would the results be the same in the US?

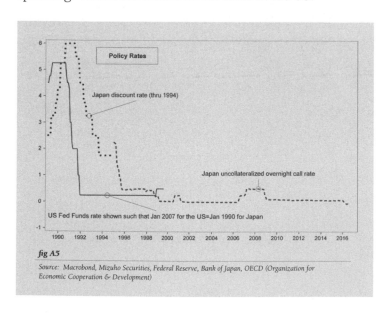

fig A5

Source: *Macrobond, Mizuho Securities, Federal Reserve, Bank of Japan, OECD (Organization for Economic Cooperation & Development)*

Aging Population Is a Reflection of Excess Supply

Japan's demographic problems are well documented, but the population is also aging in the US. This demographic problem is best depicted by the dependency ratio, which measures the number of people 65 and older relative to the total population aged 15 to 64. In other words, the (older) part of the population is dependent on the tax revenue obtained from the (younger) working population. In both countries the dependency ratio is on the rise.

Some Notable Differences

Commercial Real Estate vs. Residential Real Estate

In 1990–1991 the Japanese bubble-burst was triggered by a combination of BOJ rate hikes and Ministry of Finance limits on real estate lending from 1989–1990. However, the Japanese bubble was concentrated in commercial real estate, while the US financial crisis of 2007–2009 was in residential real estate. This difference should suggest that the US crisis would be more severe than Japan's because of the former's direct effect on household balance sheets and confidence.

The US crisis response, including near-zero interest rates, quantitative easing (QE), and Troubled Asset Relief Program funding (TARP), was substantially faster and larger than Japan's. As a result, US banks returned to profitability and the

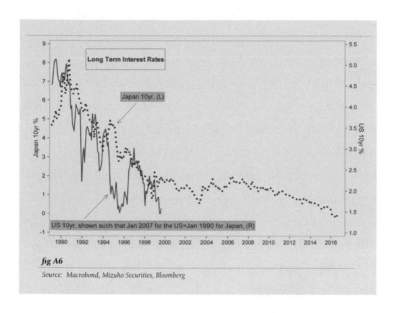

fig A6

Source: *Macrobond, Mizuho Securities, Bloomberg*

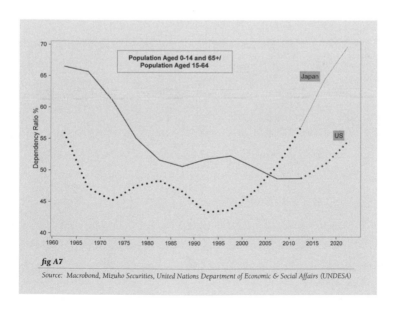

fig A7

Source: *Macrobond, Mizuho Securities, United Nations Department of Economic & Social Affairs (UNDESA)*

equity market recovered more quickly than in Japan. This difference in crisis management is due, in part, to larger, more innovative financial markets. A more sophisticated US mortgage market is another critical difference, as is the focus of corporate governance. US corporations are managed for the benefit of shareholders, while Japanese companies have historically tended to play a greater role in serving society.

For upward of three decades, Japan has also experienced stagnation, and this prolonged period has made people and institutions even more conservative. Once deflation is embedded in household behavior, it becomes exceptionally difficult to remove. The US, by contrast, is "only" in the seventh year of a shallow recovery, and evidence suggests that households would still spend if given the opportunity.

The US has a nonfinancial debt-to-GDP ratio of around

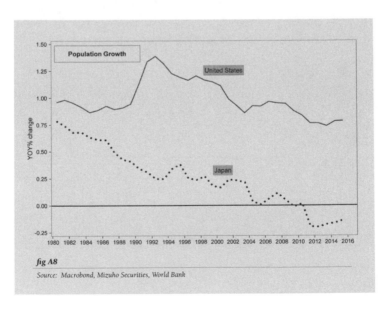

fig A8

Source: Macrobond, Mizuho Securities, World Bank

250%, while Japan's debt-to-GDP ratio is over 350%. The US dollar is the world's reserve currency. Many in Japan would say that the most important difference is that the US still has positive population growth. The key unknown at this stage, however, is whether these differences matter enough to keep the US from following Japan down a deflationary black hole.

Acknowledgments

A number of colleagues and old friends deserve to be identified for their contributions to this analysis of the fundamental shifts in the underlying economy since the end of World War II. Two dear friends, Seton Seremba-Brown and Carol Bere, have been my "go-to" team for years. They have always kept me focused and helped me to express my view in concise, grammatically correct prose. Their patience and loyalty have been invaluable to me. I would also like to thank my colleague Tetsuo "Harry" Ishihara, who contributed the analysis in the appendix on the similarities between the Japanese experience and that of the domestic economy. Harry's in-depth understanding of credit analysis also helped me refine my arguments. I am in debt to Harry as well for his data collection and presentation skills. Special thanks go to Daniel Poole, Mizuho's editor, for his fast and accurate proofreading skills and his valuable suggestions. The management of Mizuho Securities USA deserves to be credited with allowing me the opportunity to compile this analysis and supporting my efforts in this endeavor. Finally, I would like to thank my family for their support, patience, and understanding.

About the Author

Steven Ricchiuto has worked on Wall Street since 1980, working as an economist, strategist, and director of fixed-income research. He has worked at several firms prior to joining Mizuho Securities USA Inc., including Donaldson, Lufkin and Jenrette, Kidder Peabody, and Dean Witter. He has also worked in the US securities arms of several large European Banks, such as Barclays, ABN AMRO, and Svenska Handelsbanken. He is currently the US Economist at Mizuho Securities USA Inc. His academic credentials include degrees from St. Peter's University and Columbia University.